Saudi Arabia

Saudi Arabia

BY NEL YOMTOV

Enchantment of the World™
Second Series

CHILDREN'S PRESS®

An Imprint of Scholastic Inc.

New York   Toronto   London   Auckland   Sydney
Mexico City   New Delhi   Hong Kong
Danbury, Connecticut

Frontispiece: **Quba Mosque, Medina**

Consultant: Khodadad Kaviani, PhD, Associate Professor, Education Program Director, Central Washington University–Lynnwood, Lynnwood, Washington
Please note: All statistics are as up-to-date as possible at the time of publication.

Book production by The Design Lab

Library of Congress Cataloging-in-Publication Data
Yomtov, Nelson.
 Saudi Arabia / by Nel Yomtov.
    pages cm. — (Enchantment of the world. Second series)
 Includes bibliographical references and index.
 ISBN 978-0-531-20793-2 (library binding)
 1. Saudi Arabia— Juvenile literature. I. Title.
 DS204.25.Y66 2015
 953.8—dc23   2014001865

1 2 3 4 5 6 7 8 9 10 R 24 23 22 21 20 19 18 17 16 15

Teenager in Asir

Contents

Left to right: **Camels, rababa player, girl, pilgrims, oasis**

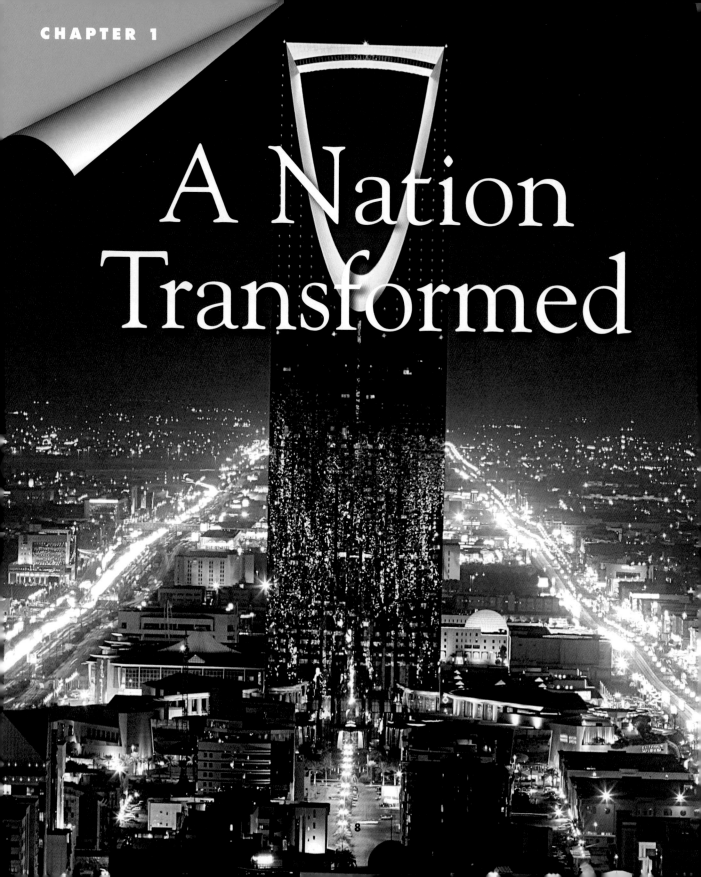

CHAPTER 1

A Nation Transformed

THE KINGDOM OF SAUDI ARABIA IS A RELATIVELY young nation. Before its founding in 1932, the land had few known resources. Its people were mostly poor and uneducated. There were no large cities, and there was little industry. Bands of nomadic tribes wandered the land seeking water and grazing areas for their meager herds of livestock.

Since then, Saudi Arabia has changed dramatically. In the late 1930s, oil was discovered under the vast plains in the eastern part of the country. The oil deposits found there were the largest on the planet. The money from oil propelled Saudi Arabia into the modern age and transformed it into one of the wealthiest nations in the world.

Within a few decades, Saudi life had transformed. Towering skyscrapers sprang up in ancient oasis towns. Industry boomed in and around the nation's port cities on the Red Sea coast in the west and the Persian Gulf coast in the east. Schools and

Opposite: **The Kingdom Centre in Riyadh contains a shopping mall, a hotel, and apartments. A skybridge connects the two sides of the sixty-five-story tower.**

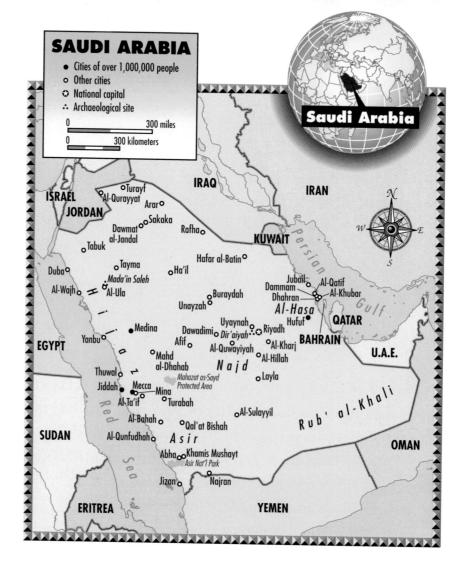

universities, hospitals, factories, and communications systems were built. Cars and trucks sped along newly built roads and highways. Saudi Arabia's newfound wealth brought a higher standard of living to the Saudi people. Education, health, housing, and employment opportunities greatly improved.

The history of Saudi Arabia is largely the history of a single family, known by the name Saud. The House of Saud came to power in the region that is now Saudi Arabia in the

1700s. Following decades of internal conflict and battles with invading armies from the Ottoman Empire, Great Britain, and France, the family, led by Abd al-Aziz, who is also known as Ibn Saud, united the separate tribes. He and his followers were themselves united by their common belief in Wahhabism, a conservative version of the religion Islam.

Abd al-Aziz spent more than thirty years working to unite the lands that are now Saudi Arabia.

Saudi Arabia is the cradle of Islam. It is the birthplace of the Prophet Muhammad, whose teachings introduced the religion in the seventh century CE. The country is also home to the religion's two holiest cities, Mecca and Medina. Each year, millions of Muslims—followers of Islam—gather in these sacred cities as pilgrims in devotion to God, whom they call Allah.

Every year, about three million Muslims travel to Mecca for a pilgrimage called the hajj.

Today, Saudis practice a conservative form of Islam. The government and legal system are based on Saudi officials' interpretation of the religion. Strict rules for behavior, dress, and food guide Saudi daily life. Non-Muslims are not allowed to enter the holy cities.

Today, Saudi Arabia faces a complex set of challenges as it continues to modernize while retaining its traditional religious and cultural values. Many Saudis question the absolute powers of the Saud family. Women are demanding greater rights and freedoms. Other Arab nations harshly condemn Saudi Arabia for being too friendly with Western nations such as the United States. As the 21st century unfolds, Saudis will rely on their unwavering Muslim faith and their wealth from oil to solve these challenges and further establish their country's role in the modern world.

Women in Saudi Arabia are required to cover themselves in black robes when they are in public. Many women wear Western-style clothes beneath these robes.

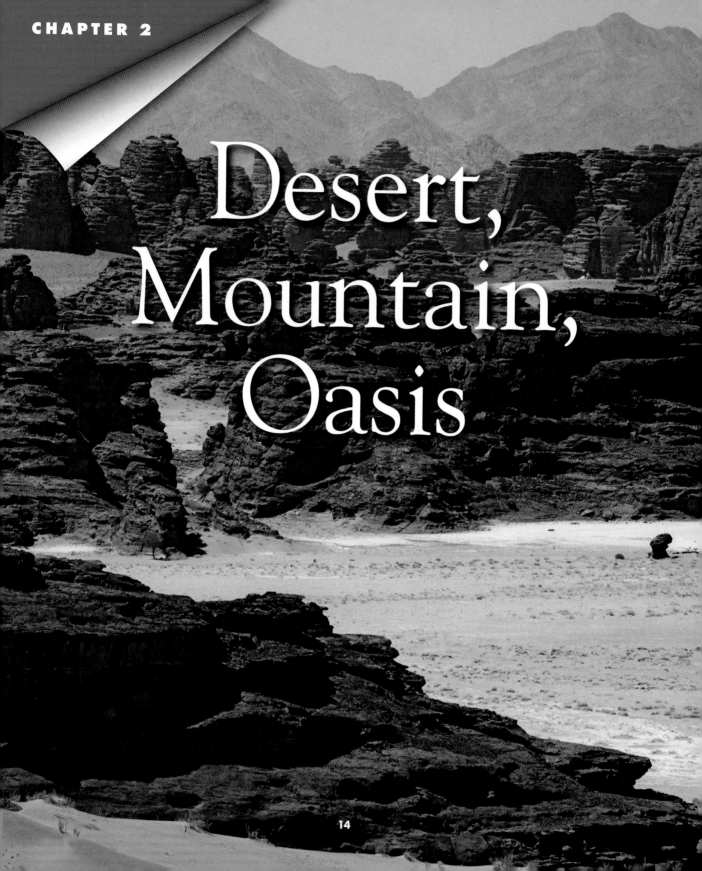

CHAPTER 2

Desert, Mountain, Oasis

SAUDI ARABIA IS THE LARGEST COUNTRY IN THE Middle East. Occupying roughly four-fifths of the Arabian Peninsula, it lies at a point where the continents of Europe, Asia, and Africa meet. Saudi Arabia's location makes it an important commercial and political crossroad of the world. Saudi Arabia is bordered by Jordan, Iraq, and Kuwait to the north. The Persian Gulf, Qatar, the United Arab Emirates, and Oman lie to the east and south. Yemen lies directly south. The Red Sea forms Saudi Arabia's western border.

The nation covers 864,869 square miles (2,240,000 square kilometers), making it about one-fourth the size of the United States, and roughly three times as large as Texas. Saudi Arabia is a plateau, rising from the Red Sea in the west and gently sloping down to the Persian Gulf in the east. A mountain chain stretches from north to south along the western frontier of Saudi Arabia, becoming wider and increasing in elevation as it approaches Yemen. Rugged mountain ridges and vast expanses of desert cover the interior of the country. With no lakes or permanent rivers and relatively little annual rainfall, this desert kingdom is among the driest countries on Earth.

Opposite: **Jagged rock formations break up the arid land north of Tabuk, in northwestern Saudi Arabia.**

Saudi Arabia's Geographic Features

Area: 864,869 square miles (2,240,000 sq km)

Highest Elevation: Jabal Sawda, 10,279 feet (3,133 m) above sea level

Lowest Elevation: Sea level along the coast

Longest Shared Border: With Yemen, 906 miles (1,458 km)

Greatest Distance North to South: 1,145 miles (1,843 km)

Greatest Distance East to West: 1,290 miles (2,076 km)

Average High Temperature: In Riyadh, 68°F (20°C) in January, 110°F (43°C) in July

Average Low Temperature: In Riyadh, 44°F (7°C) in January, 88°F (31°C) in July

Average Annual Rainfall: 4 inches (10 cm) nationwide; 0 inches in Rub' al-Khali; 20 inches (50 cm) in the Asir region

Highest Recorded Temperature: 125.6°F (52°C), in Jiddah, June 22, 2010

Lowest Recorded Temperature: 12°F (−11°C), in Turayf, in 1973

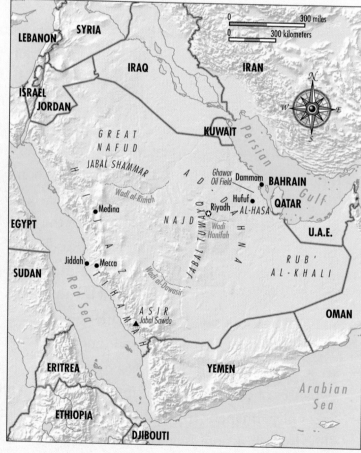

The Hijaz

The mountainous northwestern region of Saudi Arabia is called the Hijaz, which means "the barrier" in Arabic. The terrain makes the land difficult to travel, and there are few passes through the mountains on the coast into the interior. The mountains are relatively small, with most peaks averaging about 5,000 feet (1,500 meters). Some taller peaks reach slightly above 8,000 feet (2,400 m). The sharply rising edge of the plateau along the Red Sea results in very steep western mountain walls.

The Hijaz is home to Islam's two holiest cities: Mecca and Medina. Mecca is the birthplace of the prophet Muhammad, and the place where he is said to have begun receiving

Camels graze near the rugged mountains of the Hijaz.

messages from God. Medina served as Muhammad's home and religious base for many years and he is buried there.

Wadis, or short streams that remain dry most of the year, run down the gaps in the western wall of the mountain ridges. During rare rainfalls, the wadis fill with water, rushing in torrents to the sea.

The coastal city of Jiddah is located west of Mecca. Jiddah is the country's second-largest city and its commercial center. It also serves as Saudi Arabia's diplomatic hub, home to its foreign ministry and embassies. Yanbu, a seaport located farther north, is the site of chemical plants and oil refineries.

The Asir

Near Mecca, midway down the western coast, a gorge, or gap, in the mountain chain separates the Hijaz region in the north and the Asir region in the south. The mountains of the Asir rise higher and are more rugged than those of the Hijaz, with some peaks climbing higher than 10,000 feet (3,000 m). Jabal

Up the Mountain

The towering Jabal Sawda is at the heart of Asir National Park in southwestern Saudi Arabia. Asir, which opened in 1981, was the nation's first national park. Today, the park's rocky slopes and lush valleys provide a home for creatures such as baboons, foxes, wolves, owls, and ibises. Juniper and apricot trees thrive in the park, and in spring colorful wildflowers blanket the valleys. Visitors to the park are treated to spectacular views, and many enjoy pitching a tent and camping there.

Sawda, traditionally recognized as the country's highest point at 10,279 feet (3,133 m), rises in Asir National Park near the city of Abha. The city's mild climate makes it a popular year-round tourist destination.

Rainfall in these higher elevations is more abundant than elsewhere on the Arabian Peninsula. For centuries, sufficient rainfall has made agriculture and livestock grazing possible. The fertile mountains are also home to Saudi Arabia's only forests.

The Asir contains a narrow coastal plain called the Tihamah, which lies between the Red Sea coast and the mountains' western face. Rich soil washes down the slopes of the mountains, and relatively generous rainfall creates excellent farming conditions in some areas of the Tihamah. Some mountain slopes have been terraced to create more farmland and make the best use of the fertile soil. Tropical crops are commonly grown here.

Saudis have cut terraces into the hills in the Asir to make more flat farmland.

Desert, Mountain, Oasis **19**

Rich green date palm trees provide welcome shade in the oasis town of Najran.

The eastern edges of the mountains gently slope inland. Wadis deposit rich soils to create oases that are ideal for agriculture. For centuries, coffee has been an important crop of this region. Najran, located on the Yemeni border, is an oasis town and one of the fastest-growing cities in Saudi Arabia. The town has been occupied for more than four thousand years.

Najd

Najd lies east of the Hijaz and Asir, occupying Saudi Arabia's large central plateau. The land consists mainly of rock-covered plains, with stretches of small sandy deserts and clumps of mountains. For centuries, tribes of Bedouin nomads have grazed their flocks upon sparse clusters of vegetation. Some of the country's largest oasis towns and villages have developed in areas where natural underground springs and wells nourish the crops. Numerous wadis snake through the region.

Midway across the peninsula is a long and high arc-shaped ridge called the Jabal Tuwayq. (*Jabal* is an Arabic word meaning "mountain.") This region is one of Saudi Arabia's most heavily populated areas and the site of many oasis towns. Its most important city is Riyadh, the nation's capital and largest city. Deserts to the north, east, and south surround the Jabal Tuwayq.

To the north lies the Great Nafud. (*Nafud* is an Arabic word meaning "depleted.") The area is covered with vast chains of large crescent-shaped dunes, formed by sudden, violent winds. The towering dunes are separated by wide valleys, sometimes as

In most of the Great Nafud, it seldom rains more than twice a year.

much as 15 miles (25 kilometers) across. The sands of the Nafud contain iron oxide, which gives the desert a reddish tint. Nomads water their herds at the few springs and wells on the Nafud. The oasis town of Ha'il is located in the Jabal Shammar, mountains between Riyadh and the northern border with Jordan and Iraq. Ha'il is a major producer of grain, dates, and fruit.

East of Riyadh, beyond the Jabal Tuwayq, is the ad-Dahna, a long, narrow band of desert that stretches nearly 800 miles (1,300 km). This region is often called the "river of sand" because desert winds blow and continually shift the sands across the landscape.

Al-Hasa

East of ad-Dahna is al-Hasa, a rocky plateau that gently slopes to the shores of the Persian Gulf. Beneath the sands that cover much of this low, flat region are layers of sedimentary rock that hold enormous deposits of oil. The oil is found near the

Air Pollution

According to a report published by the World Health Organization in 2012, Saudi Arabia has the fifth-worst air pollution in the world. Much of the pollution comes from cars, trucks, and other vehicles. Pollution spewed into the air by power plants and oil refineries also contributes to the problem. The problem is aggravated by Saudi Arabia's dry landscape and climate. Dust from the vast desert regions blows into populated areas. In response, the Saudi government has established pollution emissions limits for industry, and air-quality monitoring programs.

A maze of passageways snakes through the towering al-Qarah Caves.

surface and is of very high quality. Oil fields are located close to the country's ports on the Persian Gulf, making shipping the oil to other countries easy and inexpensive. In the north, close to the Iraq and Kuwait borders, are rock-covered plains. In the south, the desert of al-Hasa reaches into the Rub' al-Khali, the Empty Quarter.

Al-Hasa also features fertile oases, where farmers grow dates and other fruits, rice, and barley. At one time, the region was a major producer of rice. In fact, the name al-Hasa is taken from the country's largest oasis, the al-Hasa. Hufuf, one of Saudi Arabia's main cultural centers, is the major city there. The main campus of King Faisal University at Hufuf is one of the country's most respected places of higher learning. Al-Qarah Caves near Hufuf are a major tourist attraction.

Major cities on the east coast include Dammam, Dhahran, and al-Khubar. Together, they make up one of Saudi Arabia's most important hubs of oil shipping, commerce, and industry. Before the discovery of oil in the region in the 1940s and 1950s, Dammam and al-Khubar were small fishing villages. Within twenty years, the tiny mud-brick huts that sat along the shoreline gave way to modern buildings, paved streets and highways, and railway lines to other regions in the country.

Rub' al-Khali

The Rub' al-Khali, or the Empty Quarter, occupies the southeastern portion of Saudi Arabia, stretching across the borders into Yemen and Oman. Covering 251,000 square miles (650,000 sq km), about the size of Texas, it is the largest sandy desert in the world. Most of the region is flat, but gusting desert winds create enormous sand dunes that rise as high as 500 to 800 feet (150 to 200 m).

The Rub' al-Khali is nearly uninhabitable because of its harsh climate. Rain sometimes does not fall for years at a time, making it impossible for anything to grow. Simmering daytime summer temperatures and frigid winter nights make the Empty Quarter one of the most barren and desolate places on Earth. No one lives there permanently, although nomadic Bedouin and their herds occasionally cross the area on their travels.

The Rub' al-Khali covers parts of Saudi Arabia, Yemen, Oman, and the United Arab Emirates. It is the largest unbroken stretch of sand in the world.

Water

Water is scarce and extremely valuable in Saudi Arabia. The nation's water is supplied by rainfall, groundwater, and desalinated water, or seawater that has had its salt removed to make it drinkable. In the Jabal Tuwayq and al-Hasa, underground springs create oases. In the Hijaz and Asir regions, springs and well water are common. Water is more difficult to find in Najd and the desert areas. Even when water can be pumped from underground, it is often undrinkable because of the salt and other minerals it contains.

Beginning in the 1970s, the Saudi government began attempts to locate aquifers under Saudi territory. An aquifer is a layer of underground material such as gravel, sand, or silt

A man inspects a well that is part of the Ain Zubaida historic site. Ain Zubaida was built about 800 CE and provided water to pilgrims in Mecca until the 1950s.

that contains water. The water can be extracted using wells. Government excavations led to the discovery of several promising aquifers, including a large one near the Yemeni border.

Men play in the snow in Alkan, in western Saudi Arabia, following a rare snowstorm in 2013.

Climate

Most of Saudi Arabia has a desert climate, with high daytime temperatures that rapidly drop at night. The interior of the country experiences more extreme heat and dryness than coastal regions. In the central Najd region and the deserts, average daytime summer temperatures can reach 113 degrees Fahrenheit (45 degrees Celsius), and often soar to a blistering 129°F (54°C). Even in the coolest winter months of December and January, temperatures rarely drop below freezing. Winter temperatures in the central Najd average 59°F (15°C).

The western and eastern coastal regions have a more moderate climate. Summer daytime temperatures average about

The Jiddah Floods of 2009

In November 2009, the worst Saudi Arabian floods in more than twenty-five years struck Jiddah. In only four hours, more than 3.5 inches (9 centimeters) of rain poured down on the city. It was almost twice the average rainfall the region receives in an entire year. About five hundred people were killed or went missing. More than ten wadis flow into Jiddah when it rains, and minor flooding often occurs. The city is building storm drains and floodwater removal systems to ease future flooding.

90°F (32°C), and winter temperatures about 60°F (16°C). The Red Sea coast experiences its heaviest rainfalls between November and January, while on the Persian Gulf coast, rain comes between November and May. Heavy rains in the west often cause wadis to overflow, resulting in destructive floods, especially near Jiddah.

Between May and October, the Asir region in the southwest often experiences tropical rainstorms. The storms originate in the Indian Ocean and soak the Asir with about 12 inches (30 centimeters) of rain annually, more than half the region's yearly rainfall of 20 inches (51 cm).

Sandstorms and dust storms are the most common natural hazards in Saudi Arabia. From spring to early summer, northerly winds called the *shamal* sweep across the northeastern coast, creating blinding sandstorms in the desert. Another type of storm, known as the *kauf* in the Persian Gulf region, is caused by warm, humid winds from the south. Sandstorms and dust storms can be powerful and sudden, reducing visibility from miles to just a few feet in a matter of seconds.

Looking at Saudi Arabia's Cities

Riyadh, the capital of Saudi Arabia, is also its largest city, with a population of 5,254,560 in 2010. Jiddah is Saudi Arabia's second-largest city, with 3,456,259. Founded as a small fishing village on the Red Sea in 500 BCE, Jiddah had emerged as a major port by 647 CE. Today, it is one of the nation's most important seaports and home to Saudi Arabia's largest souq, or marketplace, the Souq al-Alawi. For many centuries, the city has been the entry point of pilgrims traveling from foreign countries to Mecca. The city has more than 1,300 mosques. Streets feature many modern, upscale shops, boutiques, and eateries. The two-hundred-year-old Municipality Museum, which is built of coral, offers visitors a visual history of Jiddah from ancient times to the present.

Mecca (above), the nation's third-largest city with a population of 1,675,368, is the birthplace of Muhammad and the world's holiest city for Muslims. Mecca is situated in a rocky, narrow valley roughly 70 miles (110 km) east of Jiddah. At one time, Mecca was a caravan trade center. Today, the city's economy depends largely on religious pilgrims who journey there from all parts of the world. They visit al-Masjid al-Haram, the largest mosque in the world, which houses a shrine called the Ka'bah. Other important landmarks include an Ottoman castle and al-Hira cave, said to be the place where Muhammad received revelations from God.

Medina (left), with a population 1,180,770, is Saudi Arabia's fourth-largest city. The second-holiest city in Islam, Medina is the burial place of Muhammad. His tomb is located in the Mosque of the Prophet, a green-domed structure that can hold more than half a million worshippers. Another important religious site in the city is the mosque Masjid al-Qiblatain, where Muhammad is said to have received a revelation that prayer should be directed toward Mecca. The Islamic University, founded in 1961, is the city's largest center of higher learning.

CHAPTER 3

The Natural World

MILLIONS OF YEARS AGO, THE ARABIAN Peninsula was connected to Africa by an isthmus, a narrow strip of land, across the Red Sea. This unique geographical feature allowed many different species of animals to move between Africa and what is now Saudi Arabia. The Nile Valley cat, for example, which originated in Egypt, is now found on the Arabian Peninsula.

Mammals

Saudi Arabia is home to dozens of species of mammals. Some species have been hunted to near extinction and others are rare and in danger of being wiped out. Great numbers of Arabian gazelles, oryx, and Nubian ibex once roamed the plains, but overhunting has severely reduced their populations. Cheetahs, lions, and leopards are rare, too. Today, government conservation programs work to protect many of these species.

Opposite: **Both male and female Nubian ibexes have horns. They are longer on the male, sometimes reaching 50 inches (130 cm).**

The hamadryas baboon, an animal the ancient Egyptians held sacred, roams the southwestern hills of the Asir region. They typically sleep on rocks or cliffs, probably because this helps keep them safe from predators. During the rainy season, the hamadryas feed on seeds and grasses, while in the dry season, they eat leaves. Insects, small mammals, and reptiles are also part of their diet. Hyenas, jackals, mountain sheep, wolves, and mountain goats also inhabit the highlands.

Smaller mammals that live in Saudi Arabia include hedgehogs, foxes, rabbits, badgers, mongooses, and rodents such as jerboas, gerbils, mice, and porcupines. Members of the rat family include the African grass rat, the sand rat, and the

Male hamadryas baboons are silver-white in color with thick manes. Females are brown and have no manes.

short-tailed bandicoot rat, a nocturnal creature that lives in the tunnels and chambers it burrows in irrigated lands and oases. Saudi Arabian bat species include the Egyptian fruit bat and the twilight bat. The lesser horseshoe bat, which lives in the Hijaz and Asir regions, is one of the world's smallest bats. Weighing only 0.3 ounces (9 grams), its body averages only 1.5 inches (40 millimeters) in length.

The Arabian sand gecko has webbed feet. This helps it walk across the sand. The webbed feet are also useful for digging into the sand.

Reptiles

Saudi Arabia's harsh deserts with their simmering climates are home to at least one hundred species of lizards. Geckos, which range in color from dull brown to white and pink, are the most common. They can be found scampering throughout the desert and around people's homes. Other smaller lizards include the sand lizard, and the tiger-striped and leopard-spotted desert lacerta. Larger species include the Egyptian uromastyx, also called the dhub lizard. Adults can reach a length of 2.5 feet (80 cm) and

Camels: "God's Gift"

Bedouin peoples call the camel *Ata Allah*, meaning "God's gift." The camel needs little water and feeds on desert shrubs and dried grasses, making it ideally suited to desert life. Traders domesticated camels about four thousand years ago, training them to make long journeys across deserts and other arid lands. A camel can carry a load of up to 650 pounds (300 kilograms) for nearly 15 miles (24 km), and can be trained to pull carts or plows. A camel's normal walking pace is about 3 miles per hour (5 kph), but it can reach a galloping speed of up to 40 miles per hour (65 kph) for short distances.

Camel milk, rich in protein and vitamins, is a basic food of desert people. A camel's hair is a valuable source for woven goods such as blankets and tents. Camel dung provides fuel and can be used as fertilizer.

When food is available, a camel can store as much as 80 pounds (36 kg) of fat in its hump. When food is scarce, the animal lives off the stored fat. Camels conserve water by raising their body temperature throughout the day. Even in the very hottest temperatures, camels need to take water only every four to seven days. In temperatures less than 104°F (40°C), they can go without water for up to fifteen days.

Camels have developed other unique physical features to help them survive in the desert. Bushy eyebrows and a double row of long, curly eyelashes protect a camel's eyes from sand and dust. By closing its nostrils, a camel prevents sand from entering its nose. A camel's leathery footpads widen when the animal steps on the ground, keeping its feet from sinking into the sand.

When it walks, a camel moves both feet on the same side of its body at the same time. This gently swaying, side-to-side motion resembles the movement of a boat on water. For that reason camels have been nicknamed ships of the desert.

weigh up to 10 pounds (4.5 kilograms). Bedouin desert dwellers eat the meat of the uromastyx and use its strong skin for leather.

There are about fifty species of snakes in Saudi Arabia. The bites of the puff adder, carpet viper, horned viper, and cobra can be deadly. Species such as cliff racers and rat snakes are harmless.

Sea Life

The Persian Gulf and the Red Sea are home to a wide variety of species, large and small. Whales, dolphins, and porpoises are often seen in the Persian Gulf. Rays, tunas, groupers, and several varieties of shellfish also inhabit the waters. Unusual

Hawksbill sea turtles are common in both the Red Sea and the Persian Gulf. The turtle's name comes from its beak-like mouth.

species found in the Red Sea include butterfly fish, triggerfish, and anemone fish. Sea turtles, sharks, and dugongs, a large plant-eating mammal, also swim in Red Sea waters.

Birds

Roughly 490 species of birds live in Saudi Arabia. Hawks, eagles, falcons, vultures, and owls are common birds of prey living on the Arabian Peninsula. Pelicans, herons, egrets, storks, flamingos, geese, and swans are found along the coasts. Other coastal seabirds include gannets and boobies, medium-sized birds that dive for fish. Swallows, thrushes, ravens, and pigeons are found in oasis towns and villages.

Hume's tawny owl thrives in dry regions. It nests in cliffs and feeds on mice and insects.

Saudi Arabia's Coral Reefs

The waters bordering Saudi Arabia have the largest concentration of coral reefs in the world. Coral reefs are formations that are built up in warm, shallow seawater from the stony skeletons of tiny creatures called coral polyps. Living coral grows atop these reefs, providing food and shelter to an amazing array of sea creatures. Healthy coral reefs provide homes for thousands of species of fish and plants. They also create jobs for people in the fishing and tourism industries. Healthy coral reefs also block fierce waves, protecting coastlines from storms and erosion.

The Red Sea coastline features some 260 species of coral. However, pollution from sewage threatens coral life near major towns off the Red Sea. Oil pollution from refineries in Yanbu and wide-scale industrial development in Jiddah also threaten the reefs. The eastern coast is home to about 50 coral species and more than two hundred fish species. Coral on the east coast grows to depths of about 60 feet (18 m). But there, too, offshore oil platforms, sewage, and industrial pollution are harming the coral.

Saudi Arabia has adopted laws to conserve its coral reefs. Limits have been placed on industrial chemical discharges and a number of protected areas have been established. Much work still needs to be done, however, and the government continues to investigate ways of protecting the country's valuable coral reefs.

Larks, warblers, wheatears, finches, and sandgrouse live in the desert. The Arabian ostrich once roamed the peninsula in large numbers, but it was hunted to extinction by the mid-twentieth century. The meat of the birds was eaten, and their skin was used to make clothing. In the 1990s, the Saudi National Wildlife Research Center began breeding red-necked ostriches, a close relative of the Arabian ostrich. The young ostriches were then released into protected areas in the wild. Ostrich chicks were also imported from the African country of Sudan to add to the ostrich population.

Insects

Swarms of locusts have been a common occurrence in Africa and the Arabian Peninsula for thousands of years. Jewish, Christian, and Muslim texts describe plagues of locusts that

A swarm of locusts fills the sky. Locusts swarm when their area becomes too crowded.

laid waste to crops and spread diseases to humans. To this day, locusts are a problem in Saudi Arabia. Swarms of these hearty insects can fly as far as 1,500 miles (2,400 km) without stopping. The largest swarm on record covered 400 square miles (1,000 sq km) and was made up of forty billion locusts. In 2013, Saudi officials reported that ten swarms of forty to eighty million locusts each were headed toward Saudi Arabia on their migration from Sudan to Egypt. Officials warned people that eating the insects—considered a tasty treat by Bedouin—could be especially dangerous because the locusts may have been sprayed with insecticide.

Like everywhere else on Earth, insects are widespread in Saudi Arabia. Scorpions, spiders, ants, and beetles live throughout the kingdom. Cockroaches, termites, flies, bees, and wasps are common pests.

About 130 species of butterflies live in Saudi Arabia. Most of the species live in the mountainous regions and lowlands of the west and southwest. There, visitors can catch glimpses of colorful butterflies such as the blue pansy, the yellow patch, and the painted lady. Some species have adapted to the harsh conditions of the desert. Leopard butterflies and desert white butterflies are found in the heart of the Rub' al-Khali.

Plant Life

Despite Saudi Arabia's large size, only 2,200 species of plants grow there. About 45 percent of those are endangered or rare because of poor soil, overgrazing by livestock, and a lack of rainfall. Many plant species have adapted to the harsh desert

National Emblem

The Saudi national emblem shows a date palm tree with swords crossed below it. Saudi Arabia is believed to be the birthplace of the date palm tree, which is now grown in many regions around the world. More than three hundred varieties of the delicious fruit grow in Saudi Arabia, the second-largest producer of dates in the world.

Besides producing fruit, the date palm has also played important religious and cultural roles in Saudi society. The branches and leaves of the tree have often provided shade from the hot desert sun. Parts of the tree were used to build roofs for desert huts and baskets in which fruit growers gathered their crops. Muhammad's original mosque in Medina was constructed with the trunks of the tree, and it is said that he often lived on nothing but dates and water. Today, al-Hasa is the largest date-producing region in Saudi Arabia.

conditions of little water and intense heat. Some plants can store water. Others can take nourishment from salty water. Plants with spiny or needlelike leaves have reduced leaf surface area. This enables the plants to lose less water from evaporation. In the desert, sheep and goats graze on the *arfaj* bush and *tkumam*, a type of grass. Camels munch on the *rimth* salt bush, which provides the animal with the salt it needs to survive.

Tamarisk trees are planted along the edge of the desert to provide shelter from the wind and to prevent soil erosion in cultivated areas. The tamarisk has long roots that grow deep into the ground, enabling it to tap natural water supplies far below the surface.

During the cooler, wetter season of November through April, the desert turns green almost overnight as seeds spring to life. Wildflowers sprout, emerging from the hillsides of the eastern lowlands, wadis, and desert mounds. Wild irises, desert hyacinths, scarlet pimpernels, and golden senecios blossom throughout the wadis. Along the mountains near the Red Sea north of Yemen, white irises, orchids, and Ethiopian roses burst with brilliant colors.

The Asir region is home to Saudi Arabia's only forests. Wild olive trees as well as junipers and other evergreens grow along the mountainsides.

Traditionally, plants have played an important role in nomadic communities. The sturdy, water-resistant wood of some plants has been used to build houses and tent poles. People collect gum from acacia trees to use as a sweetener in foods or as an ingredient in ink. Some plants were chewed as a mouth cleanser, and even today chemicals taken from those plants are used to manufacture toothpaste. People also used the sap of plants to manufacture perfumes.

Bedouin still use plants and spices to cure illnesses and ailments. A type of sumac is used to treat coughs, while senna is used to ease stomach disorders. The caper bush is used to treat aches in the joints, rose of Jericho to ease the pain of childbirth, and aloe to heal sunburns and rashes.

Many different kinds of aloe grow in Saudi Arabia. The Arabian aloe flowers with a red spiky bloom.

CHAPTER 4

The Birth of the Kingdom

THE EARLIEST KNOWN INHABITANTS OF THE ARABIAN Peninsula lived on the coast of the Persian Gulf, north of present-day Dhahran, in a small farming community, about 5000 BCE. Most of the region's early inhabitants, however, were nomads, who moved from place to place. Archaeological evidence indicates they came from regions that are now Iraq and Jordan.

From about 8000 to 1000 BCE, much of Arabia had a moderate climate, with more rainfall, rivers, and vegetation than it has now. Over time, the climate changed, and the desert crept into what had been more fertile areas.

The Growth of Trade

By 3000 BCE, people living on the coasts had established a robust trade with Egypt to the west and civilizations to the north in Mesopotamia, in what is now Iraq. People traded agricultural products, textiles, gold, and spices.

People living in the drier, desertlike conditions of Arabia's interior regions experienced a different lifestyle. Most were nomadic or seminomadic herders or farmers. Camels were common livestock, as they are today. About 1000 BCE, the camel saddle was invented. This allowed camels to carry large loads across the vast desert. At last, the doors to trade were opened to the people of the peninsula's interior.

Trade across Arabia boomed. Merchants traded enslaved people and ivory from Africa; spices from India; and jewels and gold from nearby regions. Caravan routes connected

The North Arabian camel saddle was introduced around 500 BCE. Its design proved extremely useful because it allowed soldiers to fight on camelback.

Ruins of the ancient dam at Marib still stand.

southern and western Arabia to Syria, Egypt, and other places in the Middle East. As trade developed, cities began to appear on the coasts and in the interior. Some of these towns became religious and cultural centers.

Early Civilizations

The earliest kingdom in Arabia was Saba, formed in the 8th century BCE in southwestern Arabia and what is now Yemen. The Sabaeans developed a vast trade network with faraway lands and controlled shipping in the Red Sea. They were technologically advanced, building impressive religious structures and irrigation systems. Their massive dam at Marib controlled the flow of the Adhannah River and irrigated more than 4,000 acres (1,600 hectares). As defense against raiders, the Sabaeans constructed cities with castles and protective walls. By the fourth century CE, Saba was in decline. By the seventh century, the Sabaeans fell to invading Abyssinian and Persian armies.

Several other kingdoms also ruled in the region. The Nabataeans were a rich and powerful people who ruled northern Arabia and the eastern shore of the Red Sea from about 350 BCE to 106 CE. The Nabataeans developed lengthy trade routes, a legal system, and a strong military. From the early fourth century CE through the sixth century CE, the Lakhmids, a Bedouin tribal kingdom, ruled along the Persian Gulf coast. The Ghassanids were a group of south Arabian Christian tribes that controlled the northwestern part of the Arabian Peninsula. They were governed by the rulers of the Byzantine Empire, based in what is now Turkey.

The Rise of Mecca

By 400 CE, Mecca had become a permanent settlement. The city had already been known for being the home of an unusual artifact: a black stone meteorite in the shape of a cube, about 12 inches (30 cm) across. The stone was housed in a pagan temple called the Ka'bah,

Early Kingdoms

— Present-day Saudi Arabia

Sabaean kingdom, 700 BCE–400 CE

Nabataean kingdom, 350 BCE–106 CE

Lakhmid kingdom, 300–602 CE

Ghassanid kingdom, 500–600 CE

which was a site for religious pilgrimages. Idols to more than three hundred gods were also kept in the Ka'bah.

In the fifth century, the Quraysh people from the deserts of northern Arabia formed a trading alliance in Mecca. The Quraysh developed trade relations with Egypt, Persia, Ethiopia, and the faraway Byzantine Empire. The Quraysh provided protection for the caravans of traders that traveled through the central Hijaz. Recognizing the religious importance of Mecca, they also encouraged pilgrimages to the city. They levied taxes to provide food and drink to the annual migration of pilgrims to Mecca. By the mid-sixth century, Mecca had become a wealthy town and an important trading center, and a religious stronghold.

The Birth and Spread of Islam

Around 570 CE, a young boy was born into a powerful family in Mecca. The youngster's given name is not known, but in later years he was called Muhammad, meaning "highly

قربان ايدمى وفدا ايليه يم ددى عهد اتكى ونذرقليى
اندا ونه كليى د ورت يكا كثيلر ويربدى ولوكثيدرقزلن

Before the birth of Muhammad, the Ka'bah was a pagan shrine. People from throughout the Arabian Peninsula made pilgrimages to it.

praised." Growing up in Mecca, Muhammad was exposed to many religious faiths, including Judaism, Christianity, and pagan religions. One evening, while spending the night alone in a hillside cave near Mecca, Muhammad is said to have received a vision of the angel Gabriel. Muslims believe that over the following years, Muhammad received many revelations from the angel.

In 610, Muhammad began to preach what he said the angel had revealed to him. Muhammad told Meccans that there was only one god rather than many. It was the same god worshipped by Jews and Christians. The Arabic word for God is *Allah*. Muhammad told the people of Mecca to abandon their many gods and accept Allah as their true god.

Muhammad's beliefs angered many of Mecca's Quraysh leaders. Without many gods and idol worship, they would lose their income from pilgrimages. In 622, the city elders drove Muhammad out of Mecca. He and several followers found refuge in Medina, to the north. Muhammad's flight is known as the Hijrah, meaning "emigration" in Arabic. Muslims consider this the birth of Islam, so 622 is the first year of the Islamic calendar.

Muhammad gained many converts among the people of his new home. Mecca and Medina soon became locked in a power struggle. For several years, Muhammad's armies attacked Meccan caravans and battled against Quraysh forces. In 630, Muhammad marched into Mecca with an army of ten thousand Islamic fighters. City leaders surrendered peacefully. Both Mecca and Medina became sacred centers of the young religion. The pagan Ka'bah was made into the holy shrine of Allah. Tribes throughout the region came to Mecca and converted to Islam. They accepted Allah as their only god, and Muhammad as his prophet. By the time Muhammad died in 632, most of the Arabian Peninsula—including the Hijaz, Najd, and most of the east and south—was united under Islamic rule.

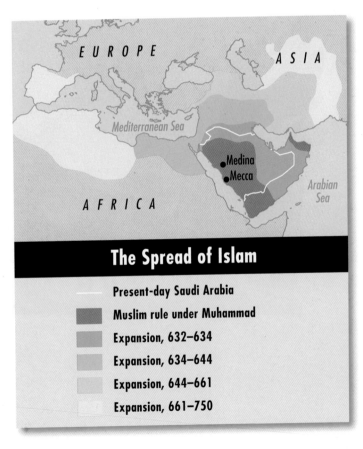

The Spread of Islam

- —— Present-day Saudi Arabia
- Muslim rule under Muhammad
- Expansion, 632–634
- Expansion, 634–644
- Expansion, 644–661
- Expansion, 661–750

The Era of Conquest
In the years after Muhammad's death, Muhammad's successors, called caliphs, began to spread Islam beyond Arabia. Abu Bakr,

who became caliph when Muhammad died, led Islam's expansion into what are now Iraq and Syria. His successor, Caliph Umar, later conquered Egypt and Persia (present-day Iran). Later caliphs ruled armies that conquered Spain and North Africa to the west, and Afghanistan and parts of India and central Asia to the north and east.

In 661, the Umayyad clan, based in Syria, to the north of Arabia, took control of the caliphate, the Islamic religious leadership. The Umayyads appointed governors to control local sections of the empire. As a result, the ties between the Arabian Peninsula and conquered territories weakened. Conflicts arose among the Arab peoples in Arabia.

In 750, the Abbasids, based in Baghdad, in what is now Iraq, seized control of the caliphate from the Umayyads. The Abbasids moved the headquarters of the Muslim empire from Damascus to Baghdad. The Abbasids, however, were unable to govern their vast empire. Instead, a separate individual state governed each major geographical region. By 972, three rival caliphs operated in three different regions: Baghdad, Egypt, and Spain.

Despite the political disorder, Mecca and Medina continued to thrive as cultural and religious centers. Jiddah became the region's major trading port and the most important port of entry for pilgrims.

Turkish Mamluk princes took control of Egypt in 1250 and claimed the Hijaz as a province. When the Ottoman Empire, based in Turkey, conquered Egypt in 1517, it took control of the Hijaz. The Ottomans allowed the tribal leaders of Mecca to maintain control of the twin holy cities and Jiddah. The Ottomans also gained most of the Arabian Peninsula, as well as present-day Yemen and Oman. After seizing the area that is now Iraq, the Ottomans controlled the trade waterways of both the Persian Gulf and the Red Sea.

Wahhabis and Saudis

Muhammad ibn Abd al-Wahhab grew up in Uyaynah in southern Najd. There, he studied a strict, conservative form of Sunni Islam. At the onset of the eighteenth century, some forms of Islam were beginning to revert to early pagan practices, a trend that greatly disturbed al-Wahhab. In response, he called for wide-scale reform. He began writing about and preaching a purist form of Islam: that the belief in one god should be part of every aspect of life. His version of Islam advocated the separation of men and women in public places and opposition to worshipping individuals. Al-Wahhab's

Dir'aiyah

Dir'aiyah was the original home of the Saud family and the capital of the first Saudi dynasty, which lasted from 1744 until 1818. The city lies about 18 miles (29 km) north of Riyadh, on the sides of a narrow valley called Wadi Hanifah. The ruins of the old city, which was founded in 1446, are one of the kingdom's most popular archaeological sites. The surviving structures include palaces, a city wall, and the Mosque of Sheik Muhammad ibn Abd al-Wahhab.

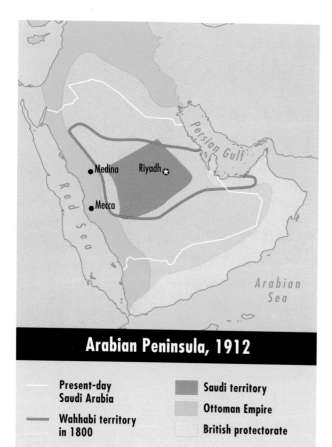

Arabian Peninsula, 1912

- —— Present-day Saudi Arabia
- —— Wahhabi territory in 1800
- ▮ Saudi territory
- ▮ Ottoman Empire
- ▮ British protectorate

message alarmed many people, and he was driven from Uyaynah. He found refuge in Dir'aiyah, near present-day Riyadh.

There he met Muhammad ibn Saud, the town's tribal chief, who greeted the newcomer warmly and embraced his purist philosophy. In 1744, the two men agreed to work together to create a state based on strict Islamic principles. Driven by Wahhabist doctrines, Ibn Saud and his armies marched upon towns and villages throughout Najd. Their conquests united the tribes of Najd and established Wahhabism as the main form of Islam there. The al-Saud clan became the dominant political force in the region.

The Wahabbis (on foot) fought the Ottomans (on horseback) for decades to create a kingdom from the lands on the Arabian Peninsula.

In later years, Saudi Wahhabi followers stormed northward into what is now Iraq and westward to the Hijaz. They conquered Mecca in 1806, but lost it again seven years later in a fight with Ottoman troops. Chasing the Saudis back eastward, the Ottomans took control of Najd. In 1818, they destroyed Dir'aiyah. Turki bin Abdullah, a Saudi tribal chief, escaped the Ottoman conquest and went into hiding with his troops in the south of the peninsula. In 1821, he recaptured Dir'aiyah from the Ottomans and then went on to retake Riyadh. Turki completed his conquest of Najd in 1824 and established Riyadh as the Saudi

Abd al-Aziz's army rode camels into battle against the Ottomans.

capital city. For a time, Turki and his successors brought peace and unity to his loose federation of tribes.

But by 1891, the Rashids, from the northern province of Jabal Shammar, had captured Riyadh and driven the al-Saud clan from Najd. It appeared that Saudi rule in the region had finally ended. The remaining Saudis retreated to Kuwait at the northern end of the Persian Gulf. Among them was Abd ar-Rahman. It would ultimately be Abd ar-Rahman's son Abd al-Aziz, often called Ibn Saud, who would transform the region into a powerful kingdom.

The Birth of a Nation

On January 2, 1902, when he was twenty-one years old, Abd al-Aziz led a small group of forces in a dramatic raid on the Riyadh headquarters of the Rashid clan. Within hours, the city fell to

Abd al-Aziz. Yet to realize his dream of unifying all the people of the Arabian Peninsula, Abd al-Aziz had to accomplish two goals: He had to rid Arabia of the Ottomans and he had to defeat rival clans who controlled various regions of the peninsula.

By 1913, his armies defeated the Ottomans in the Persian Gulf coast region, thereby gaining control of the eastern part of the peninsula. The Ottomans, however, still held the Hijaz. When World War I erupted in 1914, people in the Hijaz allied themselves with the British to fight the Ottomans. Hussein bin Ali, the leader of Mecca, joined forces with British captain Thomas Edward Lawrence, known as Lawrence of Arabia. In 1916, the Arabs blew up the railway near Yanbu, on the Red Sea, and the Ottomans were cut off from the Hijaz. Hussein bin Ali became king of the region.

Abd al-Aziz needed to defeat Hussein to gain control of the entire peninsula. He crushed Hussein's army in 1919, and by 1924 he controlled the Hijaz. Two years later, Abd al-Aziz declared himself king of the Hijaz and sultan of Najd. On September 18, 1932, Abd al-Aziz proclaimed the union of the two regions into the Kingdom of Saudi Arabia. He immediately began establishing a centralized rule and sought to end local fighting. Then he began work to modernize the nation as a growing regional power.

Into the Modern Era

In 1933, Abd al-Aziz's government granted Standard Oil, an American company, the right to explore for oil in the kingdom. As a result, Standard Oil formed the Arabian American Oil

Company, or Aramco. The first large deposit was found in 1938 in Dammam, near the Persian Gulf. New discoveries followed, and soon oil was flowing from wells in the Persian Gulf, the coastal plains of eastern Arabia, and the Empty Quarter. Abd al-Aziz used the oil income to build schools, roads, and hospitals.

When Abd al-Aziz died in 1953, his eldest son, Saud, became king. Saud built lavish palaces and homes for himself and his allies, but did little to improve conditions for the citizens of his country. His poor financial management and excessive personal spending created serious economic problems for the new nation. Under pressure from his family, Saud stepped down in 1964. His half-brother Faisal, a religious man and a strong leader, was crowned king. Faisal improved government services and launched large development projects throughout the kingdom.

Faisal was also committed to unity within the Arab world. In the Six Day War of 1967, he supported Egypt, Jordan, and Syria against Israel. When the 1973 Arab-Israeli War broke out, Faisal joined Arab oil producers to cut oil supplies to Israel and its supporters, including the United States. Worldwide oil prices nearly tripled, dramatically increasing Saudi Arabia's income. Faisal used the new revenues to further improve health care, education, transportation, and communications in Saudi Arabia.

Faisal was assassinated in 1975, and his half-brother Khalid assumed the throne. Under his leadership, Yanbu on the Red Sea coast and Jubail on the Persian Gulf coast became major industrial centers. In 1982, Khalid died, and his brother Fahd

King Fahd (right) met with U.S. secretary of state Madeleine Albright (left) in 2000.

succeeded him. The new king worked to resolve the long-standing Arab-Israeli conflict by developing a peace plan. Saudi relations with Iran, however, grew tense because Saudi Arabia supported Iraq in the Iran-Iraq War (1980–1988).

Persian Gulf War

In August 1990, Iraqi troops invaded the small country of Kuwait to the northeast of Saudi Arabia. Fahd asked the United States and their allies to help the tiny nation. The United States agreed. Fearing Iraq would also attack Saudi Arabia, the kingdom allowed U.S. troops to use the country as a base of operations. Air and ground troops from the United States, Saudi Arabia, Great Britain, and other nations, including several Arab countries, soon drove the Iraqis out of Kuwait.

Kings of Saudi Arabia

Name	Reign
Abd al-Aziz	1932–1953
Saud	1953–1964
Faisal	1964–1975
Khalid	1975–1982
Fahd	1982–2005
Abdullah	2005–

Saudi Arabia paid a heavy price for allying itself with Western nations in a war against an Arab state. Many Saudis were angered by the presence of foreign troops, believing them to be a corrupting influence on Saudi Muslim society. Islamist opposition to the Saudi leadership grew. In 1995, a car bomb in Riyadh, planted by Saudi extremists, killed six foreign workers and injured sixty others. Another bomb was set off in 1996 outside a U.S. military housing complex near Dhahran. Nineteen American soldiers were killed and more than four hundred people were injured.

A truck bomb blew the side off an apartment building housing U.S. military personnel in 1996. The powerful blast was felt 20 miles (32 km) away.

The four men arrested for the Riyadh bombing claimed to have been influenced by Osama bin Laden, a member of a prominent Saudi family, who had become a religious extremist. Bin Laden by this time had founded a violent Islamist organization called al-Qaeda and was based in Afghanistan. Al-Qaeda was responsible for the attacks on the United States on September 11, 2001. Fifteen of the nineteen people involved in the attacks were Saudis.

Into the Future

King Fahd suffered a stroke in 1995, and his half-brother the Crown Prince Abdullah began handling the country's affairs. When Fahd died in 2005, Abdullah became king. Abdullah introduced major political and social reforms. He restructured the court system and cracked down on homegrown terrorism. He set aside billions of dollars for education, housing, and unemployment benefits. In 2012, Saudi Arabia allowed women to compete in the Olympic Games for the first time. The following year, Abdullah appointed thirty women to the Consultative Council, which King Fahd had instituted in 1992.

As the twenty-first century unfolds, Saudi Arabia is working to maintain a balance between greater modernization and traditional values and Islamic ideals. Issues such as women's rights, the water shortage, terrorism, and an economy that depends heavily on oil must be addressed as the nation forges into the decades ahead. Only time will tell how effective the nation's solutions to these concerns will be.

CHAPTER 5

A Powerful Monarchy

SAUDI ARABIA IS A MONARCHY—A NATION GOVERNED by a king—headed by the al-Saud family. No political parties are allowed, and there are no major national elections. The country is governed by *shari'ah*, a body of Islamic law, which is based on the Qur'an and the Sunnah, the traditional teachings of the Prophet Muhammad. Shari'ah deals with issues of law, such as politics, crime and punishment, and economics. It also addresses personal matters such as prayer and diet.

Saudi Arabia does not have a formal constitution. Instead, it has the Basic Law of Government, which was adopted in 1992. The Basic Law outlines the duties and succession of kings and the rights of citizens, and provides guidelines for national defense and economic and financial affairs.

The Royal Family

The Basic Law decrees that the king must be a male descendant of the kingdom's first monarch, Abd al-Aziz. Until 2007, each king was required to name his own successor. That year the

Opposite: **Abdullah is the sixth king of Saudi Arabia. He is the son of the kingdom's founder, Abd al-Aziz.**

King Abdullah

King Abdullah (1924–), a son of Abd al-Aziz, began his reign in 2005. Previously, Abdullah had served as mayor of Mecca, commander of the Saudi National Guard, and as a second deputy prime minister. He has promoted reforms in education, the judicial system, and social services. These reforms include health care and unemployment benefits. A generous philanthropist, Abdullah has donated millions of dollars to charities and nations around the world.

Allegiance Commission, a committee of Saudi princes, was created to determine succession in the future. The king submits up to three candidates for the position of crown prince, the next in line to become king. The members of the commission then select one of them as crown prince. The commission may reject the king's nominees and nominate its own candidate.

Crown Prince Salman bin Abdulaziz is next in line for the Saudi throne. He is a brother of King Abdullah and serves as the nation's defense minister.

The Saudi king is an absolute monarch. He is both the head of state and the head of government. He is the primary lawmaker and is responsible for seeing that his laws are carried out. To guarantee adherence to shari'ah law, the king is advised by *ulema*, Muslim religious scholars. The ulema have the power to approve or reject royal decrees as well as the choice of a new king. The ulema can also influence military decisions and affairs of the judicial and education systems.

Every four years, the king appoints people to the Council of Ministers. The council drafts domestic, international, economic, and educational policies and laws that affect the state. The king must approve the laws before they can be enacted, and they must follow shari'ah law. The council is headed by the king.

As ultimate ruler, the king is also commander in chief of the armed forces as well as the nation's highest *imam*, or religious leader. The king appoints all diplomats and ambassadors.

Abd al-Aziz al-Shaikh is the grand mufti of Saudi Arabia, which is the nation's leading religious legal scholar. He offers opinions on issues related to Islamic law.

The Majlis

The Majlis, meaning "council," is based on *shura*, the Muslim practice of a ruler consulting with others to reach the best possible decision. Seeking the advice of those with more experience and higher knowledge is a long-held tradition in the Islamic world. King Abd al-Aziz first formed the official Shura Council in 1927. The council stopped meeting during the rule of King Saud. It was reinstated in 1992, when King Fahd established the Majlis al-Shura, or Consultative Council.

Today, the Majlis has 150 members, each appointed by the king to four-year terms. Members come from a wide variety of backgrounds. Some are businesspeople, while others are scholars, government officials, and clan and religious leaders. The Majlis examines economic plans and writes and interprets

The Saudi Arabian Flag

The emerald green flag of Saudi Arabia is inscribed with the *shahadah*, the Islamic Declaration of Faith: "There is no god but God, and Muhammad is the messenger of God." Beneath the inscription is a saber, a curved-blade sword. The green of the flag is the traditional color of Islam, and the saber represents the military strength of Saudi Arabia.

The al-Saud dynasty has traditionally held close ties to the Wahhabi religious movement. The Wahhabis had used the shahadah on their flags since the eighteenth century. In 1902, Abd al-Aziz added a sword to the flag when he became king of Najd. The current flag was adopted in 1973.

laps. Its decisions go to the Council of Ministers for approval. Yet even if both councils agree on an issue, the king must approve it to become law or policy.

The Consultative Council meets in al-Yamamah Palace in Riyadh.

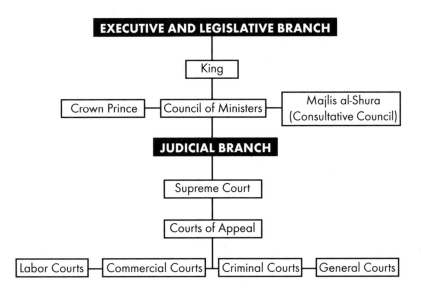

National Government of Saudi Arabia

EXECUTIVE AND LEGISLATIVE BRANCH

King

Crown Prince — Council of Ministers — Majlis al-Shura (Consultative Council)

JUDICIAL BRANCH

Supreme Court

Courts of Appeal

Labor Courts — Commercial Courts — Criminal Courts — General Courts

An elderly Saudi man votes in a municipal election. Saudi Arabia is the last country in the world to ban women from voting. This will be changing, though, in 2015.

Regional Government

Saudi Arabia is divided into thirteen provinces, or emirates. Larger, more populous provinces are subdivided into districts and subdistricts. Each province has a governor and a deputy governor. The king appoints each provincial governor, who is usually a senior member of the al-Saud family.

A governor's primary role is to work with the provincial council, which is made up of local officials and residents appointed by the king. In theory, governors report to the minister of the interior, but in practice, they often report directly to the king. There is very little self-government at the local level. All major decisions are made by the king or legislative bodies in Riyadh. Governors also serve as chiefs of the local police force and supervise recruitment to the Saudi Arabian National Guard.

An important step in government reform took place in 2003, when King Fahd announced the creation of municipal consultative councils throughout the country. The councils deal with local services and municipal planning and development. Half of the council is made up of elected members, and half is made up of members appointed by the king. In the first election, in 2005, voter turnout was low, but Saudis were excited to finally have even a small voice in politics. In the elections scheduled for 2015, women will be able to vote for the first time.

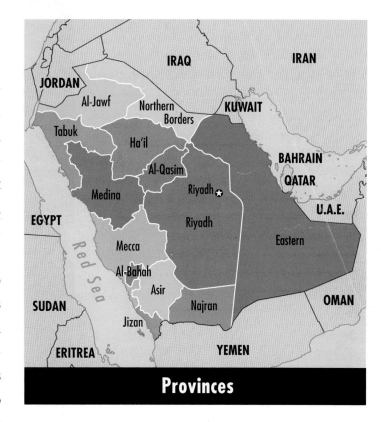

Provinces

The Judicial System

There are no trials by jury in Saudi Arabia. Judges rely on four sources to guide their decision making: the Qur'an, a collection of the revelations Muslims believe God made to Muhammad; the Sunnah, Muhammad's words and deeds; *ijma'*, opinions from Muslim scholars; and *qiyas*, or logical reasoning.

In 2007, King Abdullah announced wide-scale reforms to the country's court system. Over a period of several years, a three-tiered court system was established to help modernize the nation's legal proceedings. The highest judicial body is the

Supreme Court, consisting of legal scholars. Appellate courts make up the next level of the judiciary, followed by the Courts of First Instance, which include general courts, labor courts, commercial courts, and criminal courts. Specialized courts address specific issues, such as terrorism cases and juvenile delinquency crimes.

Crime and Punishment

Criminal punishment in Saudi Arabia is swift and harsh. Under Saudi law, people can be sentenced to death for crimes such as murder, adultery, rape, terrrorism, and even burglary, carjacking, drug smuggling, and "sorcery." Those sentenced to death are usually beheaded by sword in public executions.

Saudi law allows for an-eye-for-an-eye punishment in some cases. For example, a thief may have his hand cut off. Courts sometimes allow the family of a crime victim to determine the offender's punishment. In such cases, the family may demand the death penalty or grant leniency in exchange for payment of *diyya,* or "blood money," by the offender.

A man sells dates in front of a court building in Riyadh.

Police Forces

Saudi Arabia has three police forces. The regular police, officially called the Department of Safety, handles normal, day-to-day police activities. It is usually overseen by a member of the royal family. The Mabahith is the secret police, responsible for domestic security. Saudi Arabia also has a religious police force, called the Mutawwa'un. This group enforces the official Saudi interpretation of Islamic law. The religious police enforce dress codes, rules about shops being closed at prayer time, and bans on public entertainment.

Saudi police officers keep watch over a street in Riyadh.

A Look at the Capital

Riyadh, Saudi Arabia's capital and largest city, is home to roughly 5,200,000 people. Riyadh, which means "meadows" in Arabic, is located in a fertile part of Najd where two wadis meet.

The city was built on the ruins of an old trading city called Hajr. In the mid-1700s a wall was built around the many settlements of Riyadh, joining them together in a single town. The city became the capital of the Saud dynasty in 1824.

Today, Riyadh is a bustling, modern city with towering skyscrapers, modern shopping centers, and dozens of neatly groomed public parks. Al-Faisaliyah Center (right) was the first skyscraper built in Saudi Arabia. Located in the city's business district, the building's

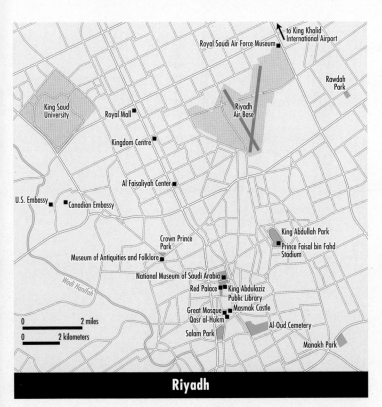

tapering design is believed to be based on that of a ballpoint pen. The gleaming Kingdom Centre is a 992-foot (302 m) skyscraper that features office spaces, a hotel, apartments, and a three-level shopping mall.

Other than a few small structures, little remains of the original walled town of Riyadh. The most important surviving site is Masmak Castle, built about 1865. The fort is made of clay and mud-brick and features four watchtowers and thick walls. Abd al-Aziz recaptured Riyadh from the Rashids at Masmak Castle in 1902. The Great Mosque and Qasr al-Hukm palace also remain from the old city. Other points of interest include the National Museum of Saudi Arabia, the Museum of Antiquities and Folklore, and the Royal Saudi Air Force Museum.

Riyadh is one of the most prosperous cities in the Middle East, and has developed into a major trade center. The city is the business hub of Saudi Arabia's oil industry and is a leading manufacturer of plastics and cement. It is also an important financial, technological, and educational center.

CHAPTER 6

Oil Is King

THE DISCOVERY OF OIL IN THE 1930S TRANSFORMED Saudi Arabia from a nation based on farming to a modern industrial state. Today, Saudi Arabia is the world's largest supplier of oil. The nation has about 25 percent of the world's reserves of crude oil—roughly 265 billion barrels. Additionally, it has the fifth-largest national gas reserves in the world. Since oil was discovered about eighty years ago, oil has generated more than $1 trillion for the Saudi government.

The oil money went into the treasury of the House of Saud, which decided how the revenues would be spent. Much of it was used to support a rich lifestyle for the Saud royal family and their supporters. Some was invested in banks, businesses, and real estate in foreign countries. Monies were also spent to improve the nation's military defense. Billions were poured into modernizing Saudi cities, such as Medina and Jiddah, with streets, schools, and modern utilities. Airports, hospitals, housing, high-rise office buildings, and shopping malls continue to be constructed throughout the country.

Opposite: **An oil refinery in Saudi Arabia. The nation is the world's top oil exporter.**

Oil pipelines lead to a tanker at Ras Tanura, a city on the Persian Gulf.

The oil industry accounts for about 90 percent of Saudi Arabia's total export revenues. Oil also provides about 45 percent of the nation's gross domestic product (GDP). The GDP is the total value of all goods and services produced by a nation in a year.

Aramco and OPEC

The largest producer of oil is the government-owned Saudi Arabian Oil Company (Saudi Aramco). Headquartered in Dhahran, Aramco accounts for about 95 percent of Saudi oil production. The company manages about one hundred oil fields and operates wells, pipelines, and refineries nationwide. It also operates a fleet of oil tankers and owns storage facilities in the Netherlands, Singapore, and the Caribbean. Aramco employs about fifty-five thousand workers, including engineers, geologists, and other scientists who continue to look for oil.

What Saudi Arabia Grows, Makes, and Mines

AGRICULTURE (2010)

Milk	1,670,000 metric tons
Wheat	1,300,000 metric tons
Dates	1,078,300 metric tons

MANUFACTURING (2006, VALUE ADDED)

Industrial chemicals	US$6,207,000,000
Food products	US$4,447,000,000
Glass products	US$2,078,000,000

MINING

Oil (2012)	11,700,000 barrels per day
Natural gas (2012)	3,644,270,000,000 cubic feet
Gypsum (2009)	2,100,000 metric tons

The country's richest deposits of oil lie in the east, near the Persian Gulf. The coastal cities of Dhahran and Dammam are the centers of oil drilling. The Ghawar oil field, 170 miles (274 km) long by 19 miles (31 km) wide, is the largest oil field in the world. Between 1948 and 2000, Ghawar accounted for about 65 percent of the nation's total oil production. Today, Ghawar still has more proven reserves than all but seven countries and produces about 5 million barrels of oil per day.

Saudi Arabia is one of the most influential members of the Organization of the Petroleum Exporting Countries (OPEC). The organization is comprised of eleven nations from the Middle East, Africa, and South America. The OPEC nations

establish quotas for how much oil they will produce, which affects world oil prices. As the group's biggest oil producer, Saudi Arabia largely determines OPEC's decisions.

Other Industries

Industrialization is relatively recent in Saudi Arabia, dating back to only the 1970s. At that time, the government began supporting development by building up industrial towns in various regions of the kingdom. Jubail on the Persian Gulf coast is home to the Middle East's largest petrochemical company. Petrochemicals, chemicals made from oil, are used to manufacture plastics, paints, cosmetics, explosives, and drugs. Yanbu, on the Red Sea, is home to several petrochemical plants and three major oil refineries. Oil pipelines carry oil across the desert from the oil fields to Yanbu.

Factories in Saudi Arabia also manufacture food and beverages, glass products, textiles and clothing, cement, fertilizers, rubber and plastic products, metal products, and machinery. Smaller businesses produce paper and paper products, transport equipment, wood and wood products, and medical equipment.

As early as 1000 BCE, gold, silver, and copper were mined at the Mahd al-Dhahab, in the southwestern part of the country. Gold is still being mined there today. Other gold deposits lie at al-Hajar in the southeast and ad-Duwayhi and Samran in the central regions. Recent discoveries throughout the kingdom have turned up large deposits of tin, nickel, zinc, lead, chrome, iron ore, and tungsten. Other valuable resources include gypsum,

Women process olives at a factory in Tabuk, in the northwestern part of the country. Food processing is one of the nation's largest industries.

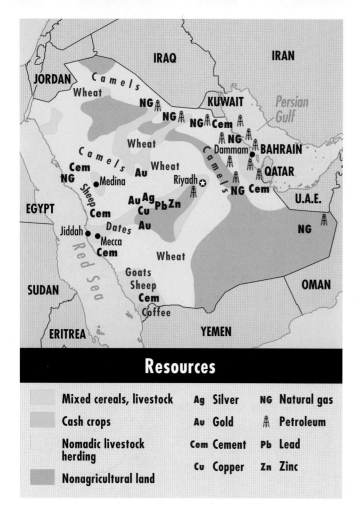

Resources

	Mixed cereals, livestock	Ag	Silver	NG	Natural gas
	Cash crops	Au	Gold	⚒	Petroleum
	Nomadic livestock herding	Cem	Cement	Pb	Lead
	Nonagricultural land	Cu	Copper	Zn	Zinc

phosphates, bauxite, potassium, salt, limestone, clay, and marble.

Workers

By some estimates, about 80 percent of the people who work in Saudi Arabia are not Saudi Arabian. Instead, they are foreigners who came to work in the booming Saudi industries. The surge in foreign workers began in the 1960s and continues today. After the oil boom began, the Saudi education system could not train technical specialists quickly enough, so professionals from other countries were brought in. Many of the original foreign workers were from other Arab countries, some were from Western nations, and others came from South Asia.

The government has addressed the issue with a policy called Saudization. The program offers education and training to workers in some service industries, the health industry, and education. But Saudization faces challenges, as officials have found that the program increases costs for employers. Well-educated workers, for example, demand higher salaries. In less-skilled occupations, such as construction, foreign workers continue to be brought in. Most of the new foreign workforce comes from the Philippines, Pakistan, and Bangladesh.

Agriculture

Slightly more than 2 percent of the land in Saudi Arabia is used for farming, and nearly all the crops grown in the nation rely on irrigation. Historically, agriculture was limited to the Asir region, the large al-Hasa oasis in the east, and other oases that dotted the countryside. The government dug deep wells in those places to tap reservoirs of underground water. Roughly 230 dams have also been built to provide water for irrigation, and more are being constructed. Desalination facilities that remove salt from seawater have also been constructed to produce fresh water.

Dates are among Saudi Arabia's major agricultural products. Saudi dates are considered some of the best in the world. The nation's leading date farms are located in the east, particularly in al-Hasa and al-Qatif. Saudi fruit farmers also grow figs, melons, and pomegranates on farms north of Riyadh. Other crops grown in the kingdom include coffee, squash, peppers, eggplants, onions, watercress, okra, and black-eyed peas.

Rainfall is scarce throughout Saudi Arabia, so farmers need to irrigate their crops.

Wheat is one of the country's largest crops. In the 1980s, Saudi Arabia began producing twice as much wheat as the nation consumed, leading to the export of the crop. But in 2013, Saudi Arabia announced plans to cut wheat production by about 13 percent annually until the year 2016, in an effort to conserve water. The government will end domestic wheat production, and become an importer of wheat to meet the country's needs. Officials claim it is becoming increasingly difficult to irrigate farm fields and to provide households with water.

A Saudi farmer inspects his date crop. Each bunch typically includes more than a thousand dates.

What It Costs in Saudi Arabia

Meal at an inexpensive restaurant	15 SR (US$4.00)
1 liter (0.26 gallons) of milk	4 SR (US$1.06)
1 loaf of white bread	3 SR (US$0.80)
1 dozen eggs	7.20 SR (US$1.92)
1 head of lettuce	3.88 SR (US$1.03)
1 pair of brand name jeans	250 SR (US$66.67)
1 pair of men's leather shoes	280 SR (US$74.67)
1 liter (0.26 gal) of gasoline	0.50 SR (US$0.13)

Saudis also produce chickens, eggs, and dairy products. Bedouin and commercial ranchers raise sheep, camels, goats, and cattle.

A farmer works in a wheat field in southwestern Saudi Arabia.

The King Fahd Causeway stretches about 15 miles (24 km), linking Saudi Arabia to the island nation of Bahrain.

Transportation

Like in many nations, large cities in Saudi Arabia are often crowded with traffic. Women are not allowed to drive in Saudi Arabia. Conservative Muslim religious authorities believe this would lead to a breakdown of traditional values. Women are also discouraged from using public transportation such as buses and trains. The major bus companies in Riyadh and Jiddah do not allow women riders.

The Trans-Arabian Highway, the road that crosses the nation from coast to coast, was completed in 1967. It runs from Dammam in the east to Medina, Mecca, and Jiddah in the west. The King Fahd Causeway, which connects Saudi Arabia and the island of Bahrain in the Persian Gulf, was completed in 1986.

Saudi Arabia has 860 miles (1,380 km) of railroads. The most important line stretches 354 miles (570 km) between Riyadh and Dammam. Saudi Arabia has more than two hundred airports. The major airports are King Khalid International Airport in Riyadh and King Fahd International Airport in Dammam. The Hajj Terminal of the King Abdulaziz International Airport near Jiddah was built to handle the annual arrival of pilgrims.

Saudi Arabian Airlines is the national air carrier. It is the second-largest airline in the Middle East, behind Emirates Airline.

People wait in line at King Abdulaziz International Airport in Jiddah, the nation's busiest airport. In 2012, more than twenty-seven million passengers passed through the airport.

Jiddah, Yanbu, Duba, and Jizan are the major Red Sea ports. On the Persian Gulf, Dammam and Jubail are Saudi Arabia's most important ports.

Communications

Saudi Arabia's communications systems are carefully controlled by the government. Freedom of speech is limited. Speech critical of the government or the royal family can

A ship loaded with huge containers arrives at the port in Jiddah. Each container is the size of a semi truck.

result in severe punishment. Newspapers and magazines, including advertising, are censored by government officials.

The government-run Broadcasting Service of the Kingdom of Saudi Arabia operates four channels. The programming usually focuses on entertainment, education, and religious subjects. Many Saudis have satellite dishes, enabling viewers to receive international stations, such as CNN. The state-run radio operates several networks.

In 2012, there were 53 million cell phones in use in Saudi Arabia. Saudi Telecom Company is the largest national provider. It also offers Internet access.

About 15 daily newspapers are published in Saudi Arabia. They include four English-language papers: *Al Hayat*, the *Arab News*, *Asharq al-Awsat*, and the *Saudi Gazette*. Those printed in Arabic include *Al-Jazirah*, *Al Riyadh*, and *Okaz*. Most of the newspapers are available on the Internet.

Satellite dishes dot the rooftops in many Saudi cities.

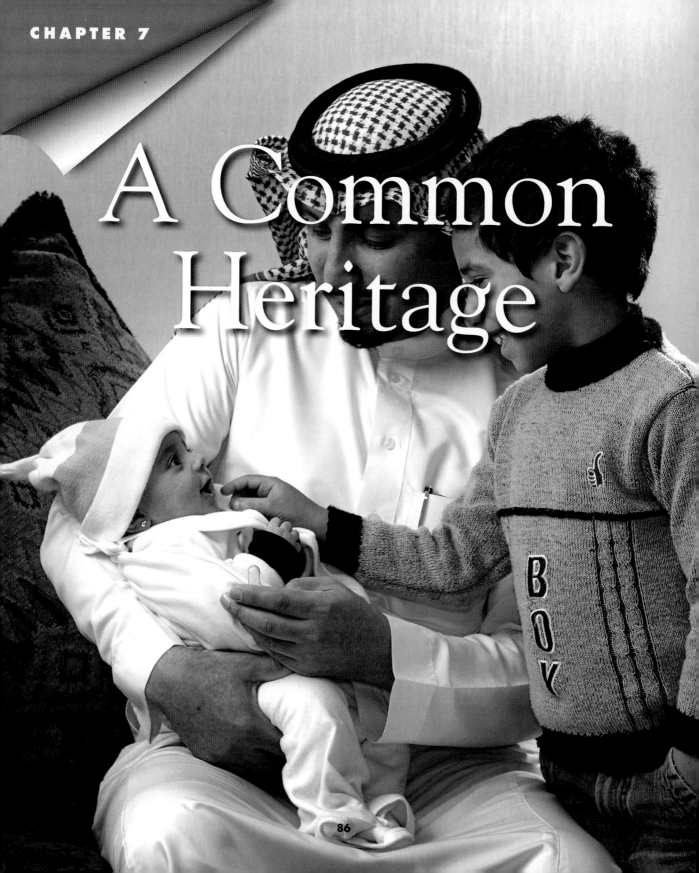

CHAPTER 7

A Common Heritage

ALARGE PERCENTAGE OF SAUDI ARABIANS ARE descendants of nomadic herders. Others are the descendants of people who lived in small towns and villages, working as farmers or traders. Still others are the descendants of pilgrims from Africa or elsewhere in Asia who came to Mecca and stayed.

The Population

In 2013, Saudi Arabia had an estimated population of 26,939,583 people. That's slightly more than the number of people who live in the U.S. state of Texas. Saudi Arabia averages about 36 people per square mile (14 per sq km), compared to about 90 people per square mile (35 per sq km) in the United States. About 80 percent of the population lives in urban areas. The most heavily populated regions are the Hijaz and the Asir on the Red Sea coast, mainly in the cities of Mecca, Jiddah, and Medina; Najd, particularly near Riyadh; and the area along the Persian Gulf, centered on the oil port of Dammam.

Who Lives in Saudi Arabia?

Arabs	90%
Afro-Asians*	10%

* People of mixed black and Asian background

Population of Largest Cities (2012 est.)	
Riyadh	5,254,560
Jiddah	3,456,259
Mecca	1,675,368
Medina	1,180,770
Dammam	903,597

Saudi Arabia has a young population. Twenty-eight percent of its people are younger than fifteen years old. In the United States, only 20 percent of the population is under fifteen.

About 10 percent of Saudi Arabians are nomadic and seminomadic herders called Bedouin. The word *bedouin* means "dwellers in the desert" in the Arabic language. Traditionally, Bedouin roamed the land in search of water and grazing fields for their herds of livestock. Far removed from other groups, the Bedouin lifestyle has changed little through the years. Today, however, many Bedouin have abandoned the nomadic lifestyle. Instead, they have settled in cities or set up camps on the edges of cities where they farm.

It is estimated that about 21 percent of the people who live in Saudi Arabia are foreign workers rather than citizens. This includes about 1.3 million Indians, 900,000 Pakistanis, 900,000 Egyptians, and 800,000 Yemenis. There are also large numbers of Bangladeshis, Filipinos, Palestinians, Indonesians, Sri Lankans, and Sudanese.

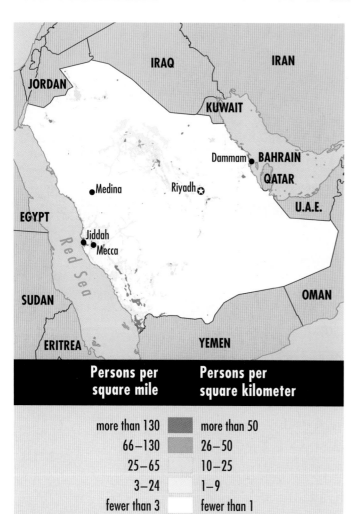

Persons per square mile		Persons per square kilometer
more than 130		more than 50
66–130		26–50
25–65		10–25
3–24		1–9
fewer than 3		fewer than 1

Language

Arabic is the national language of Saudi Arabia. The most common language spoken throughout North Africa and the Middle East, Arabic is the first language of about 280 million people and a second language for another 250 million.

The Qur'an is written in a form of Arabic called Classical Arabic. People today typically write in a slightly different version called Modern Standard Arabic. Although the written language is the same no matter where one goes, spoken Arabic varies greatly across the Middle East and North Africa, sometimes so much that people can't understand one another. There are three main dialects, or versions, of the language spoken in Saudi Arabia. The most common is the Najd dialect, which is spoken in Riyadh and much of central Saudi Arabia. Hijazi is spoken on the Red Sea coast. The Gulf dialect is spoken by people in the eastern provinces.

Common Arabic Words and Phrases

Al salaam alaykum	Hello
Ma' al-salama	Good-bye
Na'am	Yes
La	No
Shukran	Thank you
Min fadlak	Please (to a man)
Min fadlik	Please (to a woman)
Kaif halak?	How are you?
Kum?	How much?
Ismi . . .	My name is . . .

Many Saudis also speak English. They study it in school and use it in business affairs. The many foreign workers in Saudi Arabia speak a wide variety of languages, including other Arabic dialects, Urdu, Persian, Pashto, and Tagalog.

The Arabic Alphabet

The Arabic alphabet probably came into use during the fourth century CE. The Arabic alphabet has twenty-eight letters and is written from right to left. There are seventeen basic letter-

Saudi Arabian newspapers are written in Modern Standard Arabic.

English Words with Arabic Roots

The English language contains hundreds of words with Arabic roots. Here are a few:

English	Arabic	Meaning in Arabic
admiral	amir-al-	commander of the
algebra	al-jabr	the reduction
candy	qand	crystallized sugar
cotton	qutun	cotton
jar	jarra	earthen water vessel
magazine	makhazin	storehouses
zero	sifr	nothing

forms, and by adding dots above, below, or within a form other letters are created. Letters are written differently, depending on whether they begin a word, appear in the middle of a word, or end a word.

Education

With revenues from the oil boom, the Saudi Arabian educational system has improved dramatically in recent decades. New schools ranging from kindergartens to universities have been built and staffed with highly qualified teachers and professors. In 1962, less than 3 percent of Saudis could read or write. By 2012, 91 percent of Saudi men and 82 percent of Saudi women could read.

Saudi Arabia does not require that children attend school. Roughly one-third of children of elementary school age do not go to school. Instead, they work on the family farm or in the family business.

The Arabic Alphabet

a	ا	d*	ض
b	ب	t*	ط
t	ت	z*	ظ
th	ث	a pause	ع
g	ج	gh	غ
h	ح	f	ف
kh	خ	q	ق
d	د	k	ك
dh	ذ	l	ل
r	ر	m	م
z	ز	n	ن
s	س	h	ه
sh	ش	w	و
s*	ص	y	ي

*Harder sounds

Children in Saudi elementary schools study English as well as their native language.

The nation provides its citizens free public education, from elementary schools through university. Boys and girls have separate schools. Students attend kindergarten and then begin six years of elementary school at age six. Classes include Arabic, geography, history, mathematics, science, and Islamic studies. Art education and home economics are also common. After three years of middle school, students attend high school for three years. Students may choose either a vocational or a religious high school. Students who choose to attend religious high school study Arabic language and literature, history, Islamic studies, English, and computer skills. Those who enter a vocational school study subjects such as electrical skills, auto mechanics, architectural drawing, and Arabic and English. Some vocational students study agriculture, which includes classes in farm management, biology and chemistry, marketing, and languages.

Major universities in Saudi Arabia include King Saud University in Riyadh, King Abdulaziz University in Jiddah, King Fahd University of Petroleum and Minerals in Dhahran, and King Abdullah University of Science and Technology at Thuwal on the Red Sea coast. Saudi university students are encouraged to travel abroad for additional studies. Many attend schools in the United States, the United Kingdom, Egypt, and Lebanon.

Saudi students look at projects in a graphic design class. About 60 percent of university students in Saudi Arabia are women.

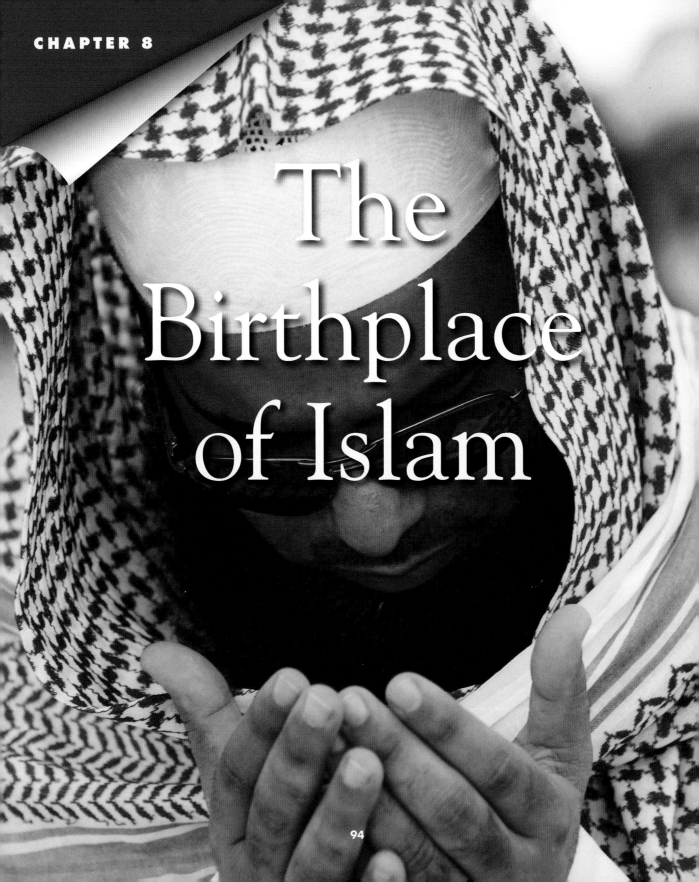

CHAPTER 8

The Birthplace of Islam

SAUDI ARABIA IS THE CENTER OF THE ISLAMIC WORLD. It is the birthplace of the Prophet Muhammad, and the home of Islam's holiest cities, Mecca and Medina. Worldwide, more than 1.6 billion people—23 percent of Earth's total population—are Muslims. Islam is second only to Christianity in its number of followers, and it is one of the fastest-growing religions in the world.

The word *Islam* means "submission to God" in Arabic. Islam is present in all aspects of Saudi society. Government documents include the opening words of the Qur'an, the holy book of Islam, "In the name of Allah, the Compassionate, the Merciful." The flag of Saudi Arabia bears the *shahadah*, the Islamic testimony of faith: "There is no god but God, and Muhammad is the messenger of God."

Opposite: **A Saudi man prays in Mecca.**

On the Islamic holy day of Ashura, Muslims ritually mourn the killing of Muhammad's grandson Husayn. Ashura is a major festival among Shi'ites.

Sunnis and Shi'ites

Islam is the only religion that may be openly practiced in Saudi Arabia, and only Muslims are allowed to enter the holy cities of Mecca and Medina. But not all Saudis belong to the same branch of Islam. There are two large sects, or groups, within Islam: Sunnism and Shi'ism. This division dates back to the time of Muhammad's death. The Sunnis argued that Muhammad's successor as the leader of all Muslims should come from a group of elites. Shi'ites maintained that the leader should be a descendant of Muhammad. Around the world today, about 80 percent of Muslims are Sunni, while in Saudi Arabia, between 85 and 90 percent of the people are Sunni. Most Shi'ites in Saudi Arabia live in the eastern part of the country, in oasis cities such as al-Hasa and al-Qatif.

A large majority of Saudis belong to the Wahhabi movement, a conservative form of Sunnism. Wahhabis profess a literal belief in the Qur'an, and unlike Shi'ites, they do not pray to people such as saints. They argue for the separation of men and women. They also believe in having a nation based solely on their interpretation of Islamic law.

The Qur'an and the Hadith

The Qur'an is a collection of all the messages that God is said to have sent to the Prophet Muhammad. It was originally written by Muhammad's followers. The Qur'an establishes guidelines for Muslims regarding food, clothing, relationships, the role of women, charity, education, and business and government activities, among other aspects of life.

The word *Qur'an* comes from the Arabic language. It means "the recitation," the act of reading or repeating something out loud.

Another important body of religious writings is called the *hadith*. This is a large collection of narrations about the life of Muhammad. Within the hadith is the Sunnah, a complete work of the Prophet's teachings and actions. It offers advice on most daily activities, serving as a guide to how to live in a righteous manner. Islam directs people to live their lives based on both the Qur'an and the Sunnah. Together, they provide the basis for the Islamic legal system.

The Mosque

The Muslim house of worship is called a mosque. The first mosque was established by the Prophet Muhammad in Medina. It was an open-air building built with trunks of palm trees and mud walls. Its top was covered by palm leaves to provide shade.

The Grand Mosque of Mecca is the world's largest mosque. It has nine minarets.

A group of Saudis study the Qur'an at a mosque in Medina.

Every mosque has a *haram* (prayer hall) and a *sahn* (courtyard) with double rows of *riwaqs* (arched galleries) surrounding it. Each mosque also includes a tall, slender tower called a minaret. The top of the minaret is often the highest point in the nearby area. From here, a *muezzin* (prayer leader) calls worshippers to prayer five times each day. Inside the mosque is a semicircular arched niche called a *mihrab*. The mihrab is often elaborately decorated with Arabic calligraphy. Its shape helps project the voice of the *imam*, the leader who stands in the mihrab as he leads the community in prayer. The mihrab is aligned in the direction of Mecca, indicating the direction that worshippers should face when praying. Some mosques also have a pulpit from which the prayer leader delivers the Friday sermon.

Sacred Shrines

Saudi Arabia is home to two major shrines of Islam. The first is the Grand Mosque of Mecca, or al-Masjid al-Haram. Within its huge courtyard is the Ka'bah, a black, cube-shaped stone that marks the holiest place in the Islamic world. Standing 45 feet (14 m) high and 30 feet (9 m) wide, it lies on the four thousand-year-old site where God is said to have commanded Abraham and Ishmael to erect a place of worship. A large black cloth embroidered with verses from the Qur'an is draped over the Ka'bah.

The second holy shrine is the Mosque of the Prophet in Medina (right). Muhammad built this mosque in 622, and his tomb is located beneath the floor. A large green dome stands above the tomb.

During the prayer service, male worshippers pray in rows facing Mecca. They kneel barefoot on their prayer rugs and bow as they pray. Women sit separately from the men, worshipping from the riwaqs along the sides of the prayer area. Women are generally discouraged from attending mosque services. It is more common for women to pray at home.

The Hajj

All Muslims are supposed to fulfill five basic tenets of faith known as the Five Pillars of Islam. One of these pillars instructs all Muslims to make a hajj, the pilgrimage to Mecca, at least once in their lifetime. The hajj takes place from the eighth to twelfth days of Dhu al-Hijjah, the twelfth month of the Islamic calendar. The pilgrimage marks the time when Muhammad fled from Mecca to Medina.

The Five Pillars of Islam

Islam includes five practices that every Muslim must try to fulfill. These are called the Five Pillars of Islam.

Declaration of faith: Muslims must recite aloud a testimony of faith, called the *shahadah*, which is the phrase, "There is no god but God, and Muhammad is the messenger of God." Reciting this phrase makes one a practicing member of the Muslim community and shows a commitment to Islam.

Daily prayers: The second pillar is the daily prayers, or *salat* (right). Muslims pray five times a day: at dawn, noon, mid-afternoon, sunset, and evening. In Saudi Arabia, businesses, schools, and government offices must stop their activities to allow employees and students to pray. Prayers can be said anywhere: in a mosque, at home, at work, or at school. Wherever they are throughout the world, Muslims face in the direction of Mecca when they pray.

Helping the poor: Giving *zakat*, or charity, is the third pillar. Muslims are expected to give to the poor and needy. Giving zakat is a way of serving God by serving those in need. Most mosques have a box in which people can place their zakat donations.

Fasting: The fourth Pillar of Islam is fasting during Ramadan—the ninth month of the Muslim calendar. During Ramadan, people are not permitted to eat, drink, or smoke during the daytime. The fast, or *sawm*, is broken after sunset. Children, the sick, pregnant women, and travelers are not required to fast. It is common to break the fast by eating dates.

The pilgrimage: The fifth pillar is the *hajj* (left), a pilgrimage Muslims are supposed to make to Mecca at least once in their lifetime if they are physically and financially able to do so. Every year, as many as two million Muslims from all over the world travel to Mecca to visit Islam's holiest sites.

A young girl takes part in the hajj ritual called *jamarat*. The pilgrims throw pebbles at pillars that symbolize Satan.

Pilgrims from around the world make their way to Mecca by airplanes, buses, and trains, by foot or camels, or by boats that dock in the Red Sea port of Jiddah. About two million people make the trek each year. Roughly half the pilgrims come from Arab nations.

Before entering the holy city of Mecca, each pilgrim puts on the *ihram*, a simple, white cotton two-piece garment for men and a white cotton gown and scarf for women. Pilgrims

Religious Holidays

The Islamic calendar is eleven days shorter than the Western calendar, so religious holidays fall on different days in the Western calendar each year.

Ras al-Sana (Islamic new year)

Mawlid an-Nabi (Muhammad's birthday)

'Id al-Fitr (end of Ramadan)

'Id al-Adha (Feast of the Sacrifice)

wear sandals that have no stitching. Next they go to the nearby town of Mina, where the Saudi government has put up thousands of white tents as accommodations for the pilgrims. There they spend the night in prayer.

The next morning, the pilgrims gather at the Mount of Mercy on the Plain of Arafat. They pray for hours, asking forgiveness for their sins. That night, on the return to Mecca, pilgrims gather pebbles that they will throw at stone pillars in Mina, symbolically showing their contempt for Satan. In Mecca, pilgrims gather at the Grand Mosque and walk around the Ka'bah seven times. This ritual is called *tawaf*.

During the hajj, each pilgrim is required to sacrifice an animal. Traditionally, the pilgrims slaughtered the animal—a sheep, goat, or camel—themselves. Today, many pilgrims buy a "sacrifice voucher," in which an animal is slaughtered in the person's name, without the pilgrim being present. Meat from the sacrificed animals is given to the poor and needy. The hajj rites are then complete. The pilgrims change into their everyday clothing and return to Mina to pray or repeat the rituals.

CHAPTER 9

Arts and Sports

SAUDI ARTISANS PRODUCE BEAUTIFUL EVERYDAY objects as their ancestors did in centuries past. Today, many kinds of beautiful handcrafted items are offered at local *souqs*, traditional marketplaces. There, shoppers can find incense burners, copper and brass urns, jewelry, silver items, leather goods, mats, and baskets.

Weaving and embroidery were traditionally a large part of the Bedouin world. Women wove tents from goat or camel hair, or from wool. Colorful, handcrafted carpets decorated the inside of these homes. Women also created other items essential to the nomadic life, such as saddlebags and woolen cloaks worn on cold nights. In recent years, hand embroidery is slowly giving way to items made on sewing machines.

Art

Saudi Arabian schools began teaching drawing and painting in the 1950s. Since 1982, Saudi children ages four to fourteen have competed in a nationwide art contest called the

Opposite: **Gleaming brass goods are on sale at a souq in Riyadh.**

Children's Kingdom. Contestants create art that depicts Saudi Arabia and its culture. The works of art are judged by a panel of teachers and artists. Scenes often depict open-air souqs, Bedouin people, and traditional weddings and dances.

Prominent Saudi artists today include Safiyeh Said Binzagr, who often paints scenes of daily Saudi life. Her painting *Zabun* shows a woman in a traditional style of dress of the Hijaz called *zabun*. Another work, *Zaffat al-Shibshib*, depicts neighbors bringing a bride's belongings to her new home. Another artist, Mohammed Farea, blends bright colors, abstract shapes, and calligraphy in his work. Some of his paintings incorporate strangely shaped shadowy figures.

Saudis discuss the work at an exhibition of female artists in Riyadh. The number of contemporary artists in Saudi Arabia is growing.

National Museum of Saudi Arabia

The National Museum of Saudi Arabia is the center-piece attraction of the King Abd al-Aziz Historical Center in Riyadh. Opened in 1999, the museum's eight galleries offer a captivating look at the natural and cultural history of the kingdom.

The Man and Universe Hall tells the story of the geology, animal life, and early human inhabitants of the Arabian Peninsula. Models of extinct animals that once roamed the region, ancient pottery objects, and rock drawings are among the highlights of the gallery. The Prophet's Mission Hall recounts the lives of the Prophet Muhammad and his family members. It also includes manuscripts of the Qur'an, paintings, and maps of Muhammad's travels to Medina.

The Islam and the Arabian Peninsula Hall highlights the growth of Islam. Exhibits begin with Muhammad's early years, move on to the Umayyad and Abbasid caliphates and the Mamluk era, and end with the Ottoman period. Exhibits highlight the accomplishments of Muslim physicians and astronomers, Islamic calligraphy, crafts, and models of Ottoman fortresses. The Exhibition Hall of the Kingdom's Unification tells the story of the modern Saudi state from Abd al-Aziz's capture of Riyadh until the unification of the kingdom in 1932.

Calligraphy, the art of lettering, is a respected visual art in Saudi Arabia. Calligraphic writing has long appeared on ceramics, metalwork, textiles, and glass. Works of calligraphy also adorn mosques, government buildings, and private homes. Saudi museums display rare manuscripts, and many groups offer instruction and hold competitions to encourage young people to continue this art form.

Poetry and Literature

Early storytellers in the pre-Islamic Arabian Peninsula were poets. Tribal poets were believed to be inspired supernatural

'Abd al-Rahman Munif's *Cities of Salt* books were both critically and commercially successful in the Middle East.

beings. Poets sometimes composed a *qasidah*, a long poem that praised the poet or his tribe and often made fun of rival tribes. Other types of early Arabic poetry addressed values such as generosity, courage, and loyalty.

In the twentieth century, the novel also became an important literary form in Saudi Arabia. The first Saudi Arabian novels—*The Twins* (1930) by 'Abd al-Quddus al-Ansari and *The Temperamental Revenge* (1935) by Muhammad al-Jawhari—dealt with social matters in Saudi Arabia and the Arab world. As the nation modernized in the 1950s and 1960s, a middle class began to emerge in Saudi Arabia. Hamid Damanhouri's *The Price of Sacrifice* (1959) explored the lives of businessmen in Mecca. 'Abd al-Rahman Munif was one of Saudi Arabia's most important writers in the late twentieth century. In *Cities of Salt* (1984–1989), a five-book collection that detailed how oil changed life in the country, Munif openly criticized the royal family. He was stripped of his citizenship, and his books were banned in the kingdom. Ultimately, Munif was forced to leave the country.

Other modern novelists include Turki al-Hamad, whose trilogy *Phantoms of the Deserted Alley* (1997–1999) is about a Saudi teenager in the 1960s and 1970s. The trilogy gained worldwide acclaim but was banned in Saudi Arabia and other Arab nations. Conservative Islamists severely criticized the novels for their discussions of liberal politics and religious freedom. Rajaa Alsanea's 2005 novel *Girls of Riyadh* is a look at the relationships between men and women in Saudi Arabia. Parts of the book are written in the form of e-mails. Abdo Khal, who lives in Jiddah, won the International Prize for Arabic Fiction in 2010 for *She Throws Sparks*. His novels are not available in his home country because they deal with issues such as religion and politics. In 2011, Raja Alem won the prize for her novel *The Dove's Necklace*, about a murdered woman in Mecca.

Music and Dance

Religious music and chants performed at the daily call to prayer and on pilgrimages play an important role in Saudi life. Folk music is also important in Saudi culture. The *'ardah* is the national dance and song of Najd. Two lines of men dance and wave swords as a poet sings traditional songs. Drummers provide musical accompaniment on traditional drums called the *tabl* and the *daff*.

Liwa folk dance and folk music originated in Africa, and in Saudi Arabia is largely performed in the eastern provinces, which have large black populations. The dance includes men and women walking slowly around a circle. The music features singers, drums, and the *shawm*, a wind instrument similar to a Western oboe.

Other regional music forms include the *yanbuwiyya*, from Yanbu on the Red Sea. These songs were traditionally sung by sailors as they went about their daily work. The music is played on the *simsimiyya*, a six-stringed lyre.

Men perform the 'ardah to the beat of drums and tambourines.

The rababa dates back at least to the eighth century CE.

Another stringed instrument used in classical Arab music is the *rababa*. This instrument usually has a rectangular or oval sound box, and is played with a curved bow. It often has a spike at its bottom so it can be rested on the ground. Other common instruments include the *oud*, a short-necked lute; the five-stringed *tanbura*, a type of lyre; and the *mizmar*, a reed instrument. Music is also performed by simply clapping.

Saudi Arabia's Hunting Dog

For thousands of years, Arabians have bred a hunting dog called the saluki to track and chase wild animals. The sleek saluki hound is believed to be one of the first dog species bred as a domestic animal. Ancient rock carvings that date back to 7000 BCE show salukis accompanying hunters. Salukis might be the breed of dog that is mentioned in the Bible. Salukis hunt by sight, rather than scent. Running at speeds of nearly 40 miles per hour (65 kph), salukis can catch gazelles, jackrabbits, and other speedy animals.

A trainer displays a Saudi horse during the Arabian Horse Festival.

Sports

Saudis enjoy a wide variety of sports, from horse racing and camel racing contests, to soccer, basketball, cricket, rugby, and golf competitions.

The Arabian horse is the favorite racing breed in the nation. Many wealthy Saudis own and race them, both in the kingdom and around the world. In fact, King Abdullah is a huge supporter of horse racing, serving as president of an equestrian club as well as an investor in a horse-breeding business. The Arabian Horse Festival is a ten-day event held in Riyadh each winter. The festival features long-distance races, jumping competitions, and a horse beauty contest.

For centuries, camels have been raced on the Arabian Peninsula. The major camel-racing event takes place in March at the Janadriyah Cultural Festival, not far from Riyadh. Camel races are held each day of the festival, attracting as many as thirty thousand spectators.

Soccer is the most popular team sport in Saudi Arabia. The Saudi Arabian Football Federation, founded in 1956, is the country's soccer governing body. The national team is called the Green Falcons. The team has participated in many World Cup soccer championships and qualified for the 1996 Olympic Games. The Saudi Professional League includes fourteen teams.

Saudi Arabia has competed in the Summer Olympics since 1972. At the 2000 Olympic Games in Sydney, Australia, Hadi Souan al-Somayli captured the team's first medal by winning silver in the men's 400-meter hurdles. Saudi athletes have also won two bronze medals in equestrian sports: in individual show jumping in 2000 and in team jumping in 2012.

Groundbreaking Athletes

When Sarah Attar (below) and Wojdan Shaherkani competed in the 2012 Olympic Games in London, England, they became the first women ever to represent the Kingdom of Saudi Arabia in Olympic competition. Under pressure from the International Olympic Committee (IOC), Saudi Arabia reluctantly agreed to include women on their team. Both women were required by Saudi officials to wear outfits that complied with Islamic law.

Attar, who was born in the United States, was attending Pepperdine University in California at the time of the Olympics. Her father is a Saudi Arabian national, which allows her to have Saudi and American dual nationality. Attar competed in the women's 800-meter race. Shaherkani, a judo competitor, was hailed as a hero by some of her fellow Saudis. Many conservative Islamists, however, harshly criticized her for participating. "I am happy to be at the Olympics," Shaherkani said. "Unfortunately, we did not win a medal, but in the future we will and I will be a star for women's participation."

Ancient and Modern

D AILY LIFE IN SAUDI ARABIA IS A BLEND OF ANCIENT and modern. In large cities, towering steel-and-glass skyscrapers stand next to mosques that are centuries old. Sleek BMW automobiles pass by farmers in donkey-drawn carts on the way to market.

In the vast deserts, Bedouin still live in traditional black tents woven from goat or camel hair. In small farming villages, people might live in brightly colored dwellings made from mud-brick. In urban areas, wealthy people live in single-family townhouses or large villas they share with family. These homes are fancily decorated and might often have fountains and running brooks. Owners build high walls around their homes to protect the family from curious neighbors.

Shoppers can be found in the local souq, a busy bazaar where vendors display their colorful wares and tasty foods and spices. Saudis also shop in modern malls with dozens of stores and boutiques. Some malls offer special services, such as baby-sitting and entertainment. The Royal Mall in Riyadh even has an indoor ice-skating rink!

Opposite: **The oasis town of Najran is known for its adobe architecture.**

The loose white thawb helps Saudi men stay cool under the burning desert sun.

Clothing

Ideally suited to the blistering climate, Saudi clothing is long, loose fitting, and flowing. Saudi men wear a long white robe called a *thawb*. The summer thawb is white, and made of cotton, while the winter robe is made of light wool and is darker

A Visit to the King Abdulaziz Public Library

The King Abdulaziz Public Library in Riyadh is Saudi Arabia's most renowned public library. The library's collection includes many rare Arabic and European books, maps, documents, photographs, and Islamic coins and currency.

The library is split into separate men's and women's sections. It is the library's policy to keep at least one copy of each book it owns in the building at all times. Unless special permission is granted, only books of which the library has more than one copy can be loaned. The library charges a fee of about US$130 (500 Saudi riyals) to obtain a library card.

in color, usually gray or brown. Over it, men sometimes wear a cloak called a *bisht*. Usually reserved for special occasions, the bisht is black or brown with gold edging, and is made of wool or camel hair. Traditional headwear for Saudi men is the *ghutra*. A white cotton ghutra is worn in the summer. A warmer, red-and-white checked headcloth, called a *shemagh*, is worn in the winter. The ghutra or shemagh is held in place with a black braided cord called an *igaal*. Underneath the head cloth, a man often wears a skullcap called a *takiah*. Men wear leather sandals or conventional European-style business shoes. They often carry prayer beads called *sibha*.

A woman shops for dresses at the Kingdom Centre Mall in Riyadh. The mall has a women-only level that is staffed entirely by women. On this level, shoppers can take off their hair coverings without being seen by men.

Marriage, Saudi Style

Marriage in Saudi Arabia is a legal agreement between the bride and the groom. The marriage contract specifies how much the man will pay to the wife as the dowry, or wedding gift. The bride uses part of the dowry to set up the new household.

These days, many Saudi women wear elaborate white dresses for their weddings. After the wedding ceremony, the men and the women have separate celebrations.

Muslim law allows men to have as many as four wives if they can afford to provide for them. Today, however, most Saudi men have only one wife. To take another wife, a man must get the permission of his wife or wives, and he must provide equally for each wife.

In public, women wear an *abaya*—a long, black cloak that covers them from head to ankle—and a *shayla*, or black scarf, which covers only the hair. Women may also choose to wear the *hijab*, a separate headscarf, under the shayla. Some women wear a veil over their faces, called a *burka*, or a *niqab*, which reveals only the eyes. Beneath the abaya, Saudi women often wear fashionable, brightly colored dresses and jewelry. At home, women do not have to wear the abaya.

Women in Saudi Arabia

To outsiders, women in Saudi Arabia seem oppressed. Women are expected to always wear the abaya in public. A woman's movements are also restricted. Women in public have a male escort at all times, and women are not allowed to drive cars or attend sporting events.

Women are discouraged from having social contact with men who are not their husbands or close relatives. This strict policy of segregation runs through all aspects of Saudi society: Women are not permitted to attend school with men, to work with men, to eat with men, play sports with men, or work in certain occupations that are reserved only for men. Many Saudi

A Saudi girl gives her sister a ride on an ATV. Women are not allowed to drive in Saudi Arabia, but in 2013 the nation began allowing women to ride bicycles, motorbikes, and ATVs in recreational areas.

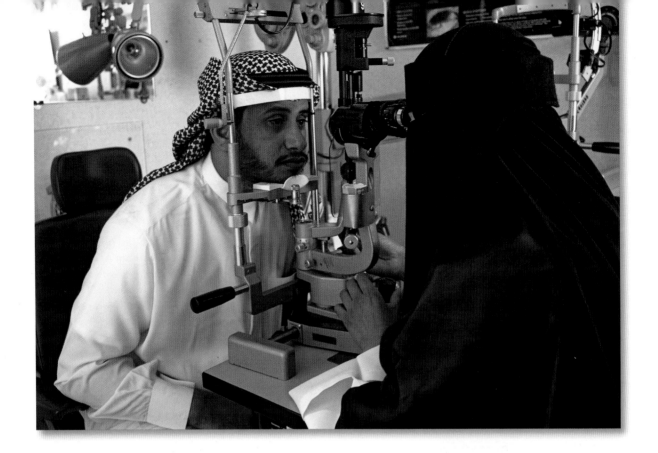

A Saudi optometrist examines a patient's eyes. Many Saudi women work in the health and education fields.

women, however, will point to the freedoms they do enjoy. For example, a woman may work in a variety of occupations, such as teaching, nursing, law, or engineering. A woman may sue her husband for divorce, although the man is likely to be awarded custody of all the children unless they are very young.

Change is slowly coming to some aspects of Saudi society. For example, in 2009, the King Abdullah University of Science and Technology opened, Saudi Arabia's first campus where men and women study alongside each other. In 2012, Saudi women competed in the Olympics for the first time, and King Abdullah appointed the first women ever to serve in the Consultative Council. Women will be allowed to vote and run for office in the 2015 municipal elections.

Food

Saudi Arabian food is a blend of traditional Bedouin and Ottoman cuisine and specialties from Egypt, Syria, Palestine, and Lebanon. Meats such as chicken, lamb, or goat are usually served with fresh vegetables, with either rice or cooked wheat, and bread. Spices such as cumin, cinnamon, and coriander are used in Saudi cooking, and garlic is a typical ingredient. Sweet treats or fruit, such as dates or apples, are typically served at mealtime. Appetizers and small salads are often served before main dishes. Coffee and tea are the most popular drinks.

A man cooks bread at a market in Jiddah.

A typical Saudi breakfast includes a variety of items served in small bowls. These might include olives, soft cheeses, honey, jams, and breads. *Khubz*, a flat, round bread, can be used to scoop up food or may be split apart and filled with vegetables or meat to make a hearty sandwich. Two favorite cooked breakfast dishes are *ful mudammes* (fava beans mashed with lemon and garlic) and *shakshuka* (eggs cooked with tomatoes, chili peppers, and onions).

Lunch might feature *shikamba*, a creamy lamb meatball soup, or *kultra* (meat on skewers) or *kebabs* (meatballs).

Kabsa can include many different ingredients, including carrots, onions, tomatoes, and a variety of spices.

Other favorite foods are *kofta*, a tasty blend of ground lamb or beef, rice, tomatoes, and spices; onions stuffed with meat and rice; *shawarma* (sliced lamb cooked on a spit); and *falafel* (deep-fried balls of fava beans or chickpeas). *Kabsa* is a dish that combines roasted or stewed lamb with spiced rice.

Coffee plays an important role in daily Saudi life. It is usually served as soon as a guest arrives. *Qahweh*, or Arabic coffee, is the choice of most Saudis. It is made by roasting green coffee beans over a fire, grinding the beans, and then mixing them with cardamom seeds. Once the coffee is brewed, the result is a dark and fragrant drink, which is served in tiny cups. *Shai* is a heavily sweetened tea, sipped from small cups.

Saudis drink small cups of coffee, usually accompanied by dates.

Sweet treats include a candy made from the citron citrus fruit; *muhallabia*, a rice and milk pudding flavored with mango; *sabudana*, a tapioca; *basbousa*, a cake covered in syrup; *qatayif*, a pancake stuffed with nuts or cheese and covered in syrup; and *kunafah*, a pastry with a layer of cheese, cooked and soaked in syrup.

Islamic law prevents Muslims from eating pork or drinking alcoholic beverages. Foods that are allowed are called *halal*. Foods that are not allowed are called *haram*.

Celebrations

Saudi Arabians celebrate two religious holidays each year. 'Id al-Fitr celebrates the end of the month-long Ramadan fast. The holiday officially is three days long, during which time government and business offices are closed. However, official

The Islamic Calendar

The Islamic calendar is a lunar calendar, based on the cycle of the moon. Each cycle is 29½ days. Therefore, the 12-month Islamic calendar is 12 x 29½ days, or 354 days. This is eleven days shorter than the calendar used in Western nations, which is based on the solar year. For this reason, Islamic religious holidays fall roughly eleven days earlier each year, according to the Western calendar.

Years for Muslims are counted from the time of the Hijrah—Muhammad's flight from Mecca to Medina. Therefore, "Year 1" for Muslims is 662 CE. The number of a year is preceded by the letters AH, meaning *anno hegirae* ("year of the Hijrah" in Latin).

Basbousa

In Saudi Arabia, *basbousa* and coffee are the perfect way to end a meal. Have an adult help you make this delicious cake.

Ingredients

Cake:

1 cup semolina flour

1 cup sugar

1 tablespoon baking powder

1 cup butter + 1 tablespoon

1 cup yogurt

2 eggs

20 almonds

Syrup:

1 cup sugar

1 cup water

1 teaspoon vanilla

1 cinnamon stick

½ lemon or ½ lime

Directions

To make the cake, preheat the oven to 350°F. Mix together the flour, sugar, and baking powder. Melt 1 cup of butter, and add it into the mixture. Add the yogurt, and mix it well. Beat the eggs, and add them to the mixture. Beat the mixture until it is smooth, with no lumps. Grease the bottom and sides of a 9 x 13 inch baking pan with the remaining 1 tablespoon of butter. Pour in the batter, and then carefully arrange the almonds on top of the batter, so there will be one centered on each piece after the cake is cut. Bake for 45 minutes.

While the cake bakes, prepare the syrup. Mix the sugar and water in a pot. Put it on the stove over high heat. Add the vanilla and cinnamon stick. Stir well. Squeeze the lemon or lime juice into the syrup and then also place the fruit rind itself into the pot. Mix well. Let the syrup boil for one minute, and then remove it from the heat.

After the cake is baked, let it cool for five minutes. Pour the syrup onto the cake, and let it cool before eating. Enjoy!

Muslims traditionally get new clothes during the 'Id al-Fitr celebration.

and business activity slows down about a week before the actual celebration and continues for about one week after. On the first morning of the holiday, families gather to break the fast with a light snack of dates, fruits, and coffee. Then people typically head to the mosque for solemn prayer, which is followed by a return home and a large, festive breakfast. Children are given gifts of new clothes, candy, and money. During the holiday, Muslims often give *zakat*, or charity, to the needy.

'Id al-Adha, the Feast of the Sacrifice, celebrates the end of the hajj. It is traditional to slaughter a lamb during this fes-

Young people wave Saudi flags during the celebration of Saudi National Day.

tival and prepare a large meal. The meat is divided into thirds. The family keeps one third, another third is given to friends and relatives, and the final third is given to the poor.

September 23 is Saudi National Day, which honors the unification of the country in 1932. During the day, many people don green shirts, the color of the national flag. Men dance the 'ardah, the traditional sword dance, and everyone enjoys delicious foods. At night, the Saudi people gather outside to watch fireworks explode high in the sky.

National Holidays

Saudi National Day	September 23
'Id al-Fitr, the end of Ramadan	Dates vary, lasts 10 days
'Id al-Adha, the end of the hajj	Dates vary, lasts 10 days

Timeline

SAUDI ARABIAN HISTORY		WORLD HISTORY	
Early peoples settle in what is now Saudi Arabia.	ca. 5000 BCE		
The Saba kingdom develops in southwestern Arabia.	ca. 700 BCE	ca. 2500 BCE	The Egyptians build the pyramids and the Sphinx in Giza.
The Nabataean kingdom is established in the northern Arabian Peninsula.	ca. 350 BCE	ca. 563 BCE	The Buddha is born in India.
The Quraysh people become important traders in the Hijaz.	400s CE	313 CE	The Roman emperor Constantine legalizes Christianity.
The Prophet Muhammad is born in Mecca.	570		
Muhammad begins preaching.	610	610	The Prophet Muhammad begins preaching a new religion called Islam.
Muhammad flees to Medina in what is called the Hijrah.	622		
Muhammad dies; most of the Arabian Peninsula is united under Islamic rule.	632		
The Umayyads control Mecca and Medina.	692		
The Abbasids overthrow the Umayyads and gain control of the Hijaz, including Mecca and Medina.	750		
		1054	The Eastern (Orthodox) and Western (Roman Catholic) Churches break apart.
		1095	The Crusades begin.
		1215	King John seals the Magna Carta.
Turkish Mamluks gain control of the Hijaz.	1250	1300s	The Renaissance begins in Italy.
		1347	The plague sweeps through Europe.
		1453	Ottoman Turks capture Constantinople, conquering the Byzantine Empire.
		1492	Columbus arrives in North America.
		1500s	Reformers break away from the Catholic Church, and Protestantism is born.
Ottoman Turks defeat the Mamluks and gain control of the Hijaz.	1517		

SAUDI ARABIAN HISTORY

The Wahhabi movement begins in Najd.	**ca. 1750**
The Wahhabis conquer Mecca.	**1806**
The Wahhabis are driven out of Mecca.	**1812**
The Saud family is forced from Saudi Arabia by the Rashids.	**1891**
Abd al-Aziz, known as Ibn Saud, begins a campaign to regain control of Saudi Arabia.	**1902**
Arabs force the Ottomans from the Hijaz.	**1916**
Abd al-Aziz founds the Kingdom of Saudi Arabia.	**1932**
The first large oil deposit is discovered in Saudi Arabia.	**1933**
Major oil production begins in Saudi Arabia.	**1946**
Saudi Arabia and other members of the Organization of the Petroleum Exporting Countries (OPEC) halt oil shipments to Western nations.	**1978**
Saudi Arabia allows a coalition of nations to use its military bases to attack Iraq during the Persian Gulf War.	**1990–1991**
Kind Fahd establishes the Consultative Council; the Basic Law of Government is adopted.	**1992**
Abdullah becomes king; Saudi Arabia's first municipal elections are held.	**2005**
Abdullah announces major reforms in the judicial system.	**2007**
Women first become members of the previously all-male Consultative Council.	**2013**

WORLD HISTORY

1776	The U.S. Declaration of Independence is signed.
1789	The French Revolution begins.
1865	The American Civil War ends.
1879	The first practical lightbulb is invented.
1914	World War I begins.
1917	The Bolshevik Revolution brings communism to Russia.
1929	A worldwide economic depression begins.
1939	World War II begins.
1945	World War II ends.
1969	Humans land on the Moon.
1975	The Vietnam War ends.
1989	The Berlin Wall is torn down as communism crumbles in Eastern Europe.
1991	The Soviet Union breaks into separate states.
2001	Terrorists attack the World Trade Center in New York City and the Pentagon near Washington, D.C.
2004	A tsunami in the Indian Ocean destroys coastlines in Africa, India, and Southeast Asia.
2008	The United States elects its first African American president.

Timeline **129**

Fast Facts

Official name: Kingdom of Saudi Arabia

Capital: Riyadh

Official language: Arabic

Riyadh

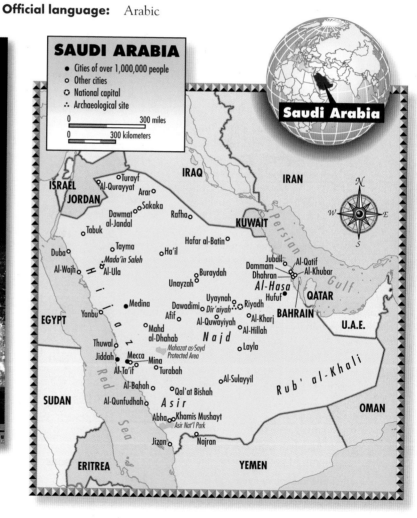

SAUDI ARABIA
- Cities of over 1,000,000 people
- Other cities
- National capital
- Archaeological site

0   300 miles
0   300 kilometers

Saudi Arabia

National flag

Asir National Park

Official religion:	Islam
Year of founding:	1932
Founder:	Abd al-Aziz al-Saud (Ibn Saud)
National anthem:	"Aash al-Maleek" ("Long Live Our Beloved King")
Type of government:	Monarchy
Head of state:	King
Head of government:	King
Area of country:	864,869 square miles (2,240,000 sq km)
Latitude and longitude:	25° N, 45° E
Bordering countries:	Jordan, Iraq, and Kuwait to the north; Qatar, the United Arab Emirates, and Oman to the east and south; Yemen to the south
Highest elevation:	Jabal Sawda, 10,279 feet (3,133 m) above sea level
Lowest elevation:	Sea level along the coast
Average high temperature:	In Riyadh, 68°F (20°C) in January, 110°F (43°C) in July
Average low temperature:	In Riyadh, 44°F (7°C) in January, 88°F (31°C) in July
Average annual precipitation:	4 inches (10 cm) nationwide; 0 inches in Rub' al-Khali; 20 inches (50 cm) in the Asir region

Red Sea

National population (2013 est.): 26,939,583

Population of major cities (2012 est.):

Riyadh	5,254,560
Jiddah	3,456,259
Mecca	1,675,368
Medina	1,180,770
Dammam	903,597

Landmarks:
- ▶ *Al-Masjid al-Haram Mosque*, Mecca
- ▶ *Asir National Park*, near Abha
- ▶ *Mahazat as-Sayd Protected Area*, near al-Ta'if
- ▶ *Mosque of the Prophet*, Medina
- ▶ *National Museum of Saudi Arabia*, Riyadh

Economy: Saudi Arabia's economy is based on oil. It possesses about 17 percent of the world's oil reserves and is the world's largest oil producer. The government has recently encouraged the development of natural gas resources. Other industries include ship repair, aircraft repair, and construction, and the manufacture of chemicals, fertilizer, and steel.

Currency: The Saudi riyal (SR). In 2014, US$1 equaled 3.75 SR, and 1 SR equaled US$0.27.

System of weights and measures: Metric system

Literacy rate (2012): 91% male; 82% female

Currency

Schoolchildren

King Abdullah

Common Arabic words and phrases:		
	Al salaam alaykum	Hello
	Ma' al-salama	Good-bye
	Na'am	Yes
	La	No
	Shukran	Thank you
	Min fadlak	Please (to a man)
	Min fadlik	Please (to a woman)
	Kaif halak?	How are you?
	Kum?	How much?
	Ismi . . .	My name is . . .

Prominent Saudis: Abd al-Aziz (Ibn Saud) (1880–1953)
Founder of the Kingdom of Saudi Arabia

Abdullah (1924–)
King of Saudi Arabia

Raja Alem (1970–)
Novelist

Safiyeh Said Binzagr (1940–)
Artist

Muhammad (ca. 570–632)
Prophet of Islam

'Abd al-Rahman Munif (1933–2004)
Novelist

Hadi Souan al-Somayli (1976–)
Olympic hurdler

To Find Out More

Books

▶ Barnes, Trevor. *Islam*. New York: Kingfisher, 2013.

▶ Conover, Sarah. *Muhammad: The Story of a Prophet and Reformer*. Boston: Skinner House Books, 2013.

▶ Farndon, John. *Oil*. New York: DK Publishing, 2012.

▶ January, Brendan. *The Arab Conquests of the Middle East*. Minneapolis, MN: Twenty-First Century Books, 2009.

▶ Reed, Jennifer Bond. *The Saudi Royal Family*. New York: Chelsea House, 2007.

DVDs

▶ *Inside Mecca*. National Geographic, 2003.

▶ *20/20: Inside Saudi Arabia*. ABC News, 2010.

▶ *20/20: Saudi Royal Family*. ABC News, 2010.

▶ Visit this Scholastic Web site for more information on Saudi Arabia:
www.factsfornow.scholastic.com
Enter the keywords **Saudi Arabia**

Index

Page numbers in *italics*
indicate illustrations.

Ghawar, 75
Ha'il, 22, *42*
Hajr, 71
al-Hasa, 23, 79, 96
Hufuf, 23
Jizan, 84
Jubail, 76, 84
al-Khubar, 24
al-Qatif, 79, 96
Ras Tanura, *74*
Tabuk, *77*
Yanbu, 18, 37, 55, 76, 84
Classical Arabic, 89
climate, 15, 16, 19, 21, *21*, 22, 25, 27–28, *27*, *28*, 43, 116
clothing, 13, *13*, 97, 106, 116–118, *116*, *117*, 126, *126*, 127
coastline, 16, *16*, 19, 27–28, 36
coffee, 20, 79, 121, 123, *123*, 125
communications, 9–10, 84–85, *85*, 90
conservation, 31, 37
Consultative Council, 59, 64–65, *65*, 120
coral reefs, 37, *37*
Council of Ministers, 63, 65
Courts of First Instance, 68
criminal punishments, 68–69
currency (Saudi riyal), 76, *76*, 116

D

daff (musical instrument), 109
ad-Dahna desert, 22
Dhahran. *See also* cities.
  early inhabitants, 43
  location of, 24
  oil industry in, 74, 75
  terrorism in, 58, *58*
  universities in, 93
Damanhouri, Hamid, 108
Dammam. *See also* cities.
  location of, 24
  oil industry and, 24, 56, 75
  population of, *24*, 87, 88
  port of, *24*, 84

railroads, 82–83
  Trans-Arabian Highway and, 82
dance, 109, *110*, 127
date palm trees, 40, *40*
dates, 69, 79, 80
death penalties, 68, 69
Department of Safety, 70
desalination, 26, 79
deserts, 16, 20, 22, 24–25, *25*, 33, 34, *34*, 37, 39–40, *40–41*
Dhahran, 24, 58, *58*, 74, 75, 93
dhub lizards, 33, 35
Dir'aiyah, 52, *52*, 53
diyya ("blood money"), 69
Duba, 84
dust storms, 28

E

economy. *See also* oil industry.
  agriculture, 75
  Arab-Israeli War and, 56
  cost of living, 81
  currency (Saudi riyal), 76, *76*
  exports, 74, 80
  fishing industry, 37
  food processing, *77*
  industrialization, 76
  Islamic religion and, 29
  Majlis al-Shura (Consultative Council) and, 64
  manufacturing, 71, 75, 76, 77
  Mecca, 29
  mining, 75, 77–78
  petrochemical industry, 76
  Saud (king) and, 56
  souqs (marketplaces), 29, *104*, 105, 106, 115
  tourism, 37
  trade, 43–45, 47, 51
education, 9, 56, 59, 62, 63, 73, 78, 85, 91–93, *92*, *93*, 97, 119, 120
Egyptian uromastyx, 33, 35
elections, 61, 66, 120
elevation, 16, 17, 18, 19

embroidery, 105
employment, 10, 37, 74, 78, 88, 90, 91, 120, *120*
Empty Quarter (Rub' al-Khali), 16, 23, 24–25, *25*, 39
endangered species, 31
English language, 90, *92*
executive branch of government, 61–63, 65
exports, 74, 80

F

Fahd (king), 56–57, *57*, 64, 67
Faisal (king), 56, 57
families, 86, 91, 126
Farea, Mohammed, 106
fasting, 101, 124
fishing industry, 37
Five Pillars of Islam, 100, 101
flooding, 28, *28*
foods, 13, 39, 40, 61, 69, *77*, 97, 101, 103, 121–124, *121*, *122*, 125, *125*, 126
foreign workers, 58, 78, 88, 90
forests, 19, 41
France, 11

G

geography
  borders, 15
  caves, 23, *23*, 29
  coastline, 16, *16*, 19, 27–28, 36
  deserts, 16, 20, 22, 24–25, *25*, 33, 34, *34*, 37, 39–40, *40–41*
  elevation, 16, 17, 18, 19
  al-Hasa region, 22–23, 26, 40
  Hijaz region, 17–18, *17*, 47, 49, 51, 53, 55, 87
  land area, 15, 16
  mountains, 15, 16, 17–18, *17*, 18–20, *18*, 21, 22, 39
  Najd region, 20–22, 26, 27, 49, 52, 53, 55, 87
  oases, 20, *20*, 21, 22, 23, 26, 79, 96
  Red Sea isthmus, 31

'Id al-Fitr holiday, 103, 124, 126, *126*
ihram (pilgrimage garment), 102
ijma' (scholarly opinions), 67
imams (leaders), 63, 99
jamarat ritual, *102*, 103
judicial branch and, 67
Ka'bah shrine, 29, 48, 49, 100
Majlis, 59, 64–65, *65*, 67, 120
Masjid al-Qiblatain mosque, 29, *29*
mihrab (mosque arch), 99
minaret (mosque tower), 98, 99
mosques, 29, 40, 52, 71, 76, *76*,
    98–100, *98*, *100*, 101, 107
muezzin (prayer leader), 99
mufti (religious scholars), 63
Muhammad ibn Abd al-Wahhab
    and, 51–52
Muhammad (prophet), 12, 17–18,
    29, 40, 47–49, 95, 96, 98, 100,
    101, 103, 107, 124, 133
music and, 109
Mutawwa'un (police force), 70
prayer, *50*, 61, *94*, 97, 99, 100, 101,
    101, 103
Qur'an (holy book), 61, 67, 89, 95,
    97, *97*, 99, 100, 107
Ramadan (holy month), 101, 103,
    124
salat (daily prayers), 101, *101*
shahadah (declaration of faith), 64,
    64, 95, 101
shari'ah law, 61, 63, 97, 98, 113,
    118, 124
Shi'ism, 96, *96*
spread of, 49–50, *49*
Sunnah (holy book), 61, 67, 98
Sunnism, 51, 96
tawaf ritual, 103
transportation and, 82, 118, *119*
ulema (scholars), 63
Umar (caliph) and, 50
Umayyad Caliphate, 50, 107

Wahhabism, 11, 51–53, *53*, 64,
    96–97
women and, 82, 97, 100
worldwide membership of, 95
zakat (charity), 101, 126

J
Jabal Sawda, 16, 18–19, *18*
Jabal Shammar, 22
Jabal Tuwayq, 21, 26
jamarat ritual, *102*, 103
al-Jawhari, Muhammad, 108
Jiddah. *See also* cities.
    climate of, 16, 28, *28*
    coral reefs and, 37
    flooding in, 28, *28*
    government and, 18
    King Abdulaziz International
        Airport, 83, *83*
    King Abdulaziz University, 93
    location of, 18
    marketplace in, *121*
    oil industry and, 73
    Ottoman Empire and, 51
    pilgrims and, 51, 102
    population of, 87, 88
    port of, 51, 84, *84*
    Trans-Arabian Highway and, 82
    women in, 82
Jizan, 84
Jubail, 76, 84
Judaism, 48
judicial branch of government, 59, 62,
    63, 65, 67, 69

K
Ka'bah shrine, 29, 48, 49, 100
kauf (storms), 28
Khafaji, Ibrahim, 68
Khal, Abdo, 109
Khalid (king), 56, 57
al-Khateeb, Abdul Rahman, 68
al-Khubar, 24
King Fahd Causeway, 82, *82*

L
Lakhmid kingdom, 46, *46*
languages, 89–90, *90*, 90–91, *91*, 92,
    92, 99
Lawrence, Thomas Edward, 55
legislative branch of government, 65, 66
leopards, 31
libraries, 116
lions, 31
literature, 107–109, 133
livestock, 9, 19, 20, 39, 40, 81, 88
liwa (music and dance), 110
local governments, 66–67, *66*
locusts, 38–39, *38*

M
Mabahith (secret police), 70
Mada'in Saleh tombs, 47, *47*
Majlis, 59, 64–65, *65*, 67, 120
Mamluk dynasty, 51
manufacturing, 71, 75, 77
maps. *See also* historical maps.
    geopolitical, *10*
    population density, 88
    resources, *78*
    Riyadh, *71*
    topographical, *16*
Marib, Yemen, 45, *45*
marine life, 35–36, *35*, 37, *37*
marriage, 118, *118*
Mecca. *See also* cities.
    Ain Zubaida historic site, *26*
    economy of, 29
    entrance restrictions, 96
    Grand Mosque of Mecca, 98
    Hijaz region and, 17
    al-Hira cave, 29
    Ka'bah shrine, 29, 46, *48*
    location of, 29
    al-Masjid al-Haram mosque, 29
    Muhammad (prophet) in, 17–18,
        47, 48, 124
    non-Muslims in, 13
    Ottoman Empire and, 51

Meet the Author

NEL YOMTOV IS AN AWARD-WINNING AUTHOR and editor with a passion for writing nonfiction books for young people. In recent years, he has written books about history and geography as well as graphic-novel adaptations of classic mythology, sports biographies, and science topics.

Yomtov was born in New York City. After graduating college, he worked at Marvel Comics, where he handled all phases of comic book production work. Yomtov has also written, edited, and colored hundreds of Marvel comic books. He has served as editorial director of a children's nonfiction book publisher and also as publisher of the Hammond World Atlas book division. In between, he squeezed in a two-year stint as consultant to Major League Baseball, where he helped supervise an educational program for elementary and middle schools throughout the country.

Yomtov lives in the New York area with his wife, Nancy, a teacher and writer, and son, Jess, a sports journalist.

Photo Credits

Photographs ©: